ME AND THE BOYS
A MAN'S GUIDE TO SINGLE PARENTHOOD

By Bryan Heger

PublishAmerica
Baltimore

First printing

ISBN: 1-4241-8459-2 (softcover)
ISBN: 978-1-61582-443-4 (hardcover)
PUBLISHED BY PUBLISHAMERICA, LLLP
www.publishamerica.com
Baltimore

Printed in the United States of America

Contents

DEDICATION AND PREFACE

First, I would like to dedicate this book to my mother. My mother raised three boys. She had the foresight to make sure she taught all of us to sew, cook, clean, do a budget, and balance a checkbook. Things others ignore in the raising of boys. I only hope I have the foresight and the will to do half the job raising my boys as my mother did raising us.

Second, I want to dedicate this book to single parents everywhere. Until you have walked a mile in their shoes you can never have any idea of how truly hard it is. This is without a doubt the hardest job in the world. In addition, to make matters worse, you may never know how good of a job you did.

There is a saying among the CIA community: our successes will never be known but everyone knows about our failures. This is true with parenthood. If your child starts getting into trouble, everyone knows about it almost before you do. However, if you are successful, you may never hear about it.

Another thing that should be addressed here is I do not want this work thought of in any way as spouse bashing. There are many different ways men are finding themselves raising children on their own. Suffice it to say, I am one of that growing group of men. My hope is that what is written here will help you get through some tough times. Help you in your everyday tasks with and for your children. If either is accomplished, then it will make it a better world for your children. Shortly after starting this project, I received a phone call from my good friend Donald. He used to work for me at the police department. Of course, I expected our usual friendly conversation. As soon as he spoke, I could tell from the tone of his voice that something was terribly wrong. He told me that when he had returned from working a night shift he found his 31-year-old wife had passed away during the night. He is now raising their 10-month-old son.

I had spoken to him about writing this and had even let him read some of the first writings from it. I flew out for the funeral to support him. He looked at me one day and said, "Make sure you finish that book. I'm gonna need it now." I hope to provide you some helpful tips. Maybe you will get a few laughs along the way.

CHAPTER ONE: IN THE BEGINNING

October fifteenth of 2003, I was ending a twenty-six-year chapter of my life. I had joined the police department at eighteen years old. I played hard for twenty-six years. Two back operations later, the only thing holding my fused lower back together was a couple of titanium rods and six titanium screws. The county said thanks for the service, but goodbye. My wife and I went down and signed my papers giving me a work related medical retirement. I think I would have liked to go out more on my terms, but oh well, twenty-six years was a pretty good run.

My wife and I discussed what we would do next. We figured I would take a few months off. Moreover, in the New Year start looking for some type of consulting work. I was also going to go back to college and get my Master's degree. We felt this would be a good example to set for the boys. It would also make me more employable. Because of the rotating shifts I had to work at the police department, I decided I did not want another full-time job. I had spent enough time away from my family because of work, to start it all over again with another job. That added with the fact we did not know how my back surgery would effect how long I could work, at what type of job. I could of course never work in any field that would require a lot of physical or manual labor. Sitting seemed to be the worse thing I could do for my back. Therefore, we agreed I would take off some time and we would see where we wound up in the New Year.

November fifteenth of 2003 my wife of almost thirteen years said she was moving out. She packed her things and left. I say almost thirteen years because November 16 would have been our wedding anniversary. Now I am sure someone leaves someone every day. That has become the dynamic of relationships in our time. What made mine a little stranger than most was when my wife left, she left our children with me. Now don't get me wrong, I am ecstatic that she left the boys with me. However, you must admit it is not the stereotypical separation when the wife leaves the home, the husband, and the children.

As I said in the preface and will repeat through this book, I am not spouse bashing. Why our marriage failed in not the topic of this book. What is the topic is how an increasing number of men are left to raise their children. What you are about to read is my story. Maybe you can learn a few things, maybe you'll see you are not the only one in your situation and maybe you'll get a few laughs and learn from some of my mistakes.

As I said, it was mid November when she left and I was concerned that the boys would stop seeing this time of the year as Thanksgiving, but as the time of year Mommy left. So I arranged for us to go to Ocean City Maryland for Thanksgiving. My parents were not too happy with my decision, but I told them I had to make my decisions based on what I thought would be best for the boys. Now as you might imagine a place called Ocean City wasn't too busy in November. We stayed in a very nice hotel. We had a small balcony over looking the large atrium and the heated indoor pool. From our room we could see the surf from the Atlantic Ocean, breaking on the beach.

My daughter Amy, from my first marriage was going to college in Salisbury, Maryland. Salisbury is only about half an hour from where we were staying in Ocean City. This may be one of the attractions drawing students to attend. We actually celebrated Thanksgiving on

Wednesday night. My daughter wanted to get back to her mother's house for Thanksgiving. The boys and I spent the holiday swimming, watching movies and generally just bumming around. Of course, it was over too soon and the boys had to go back to school.

When they started back to school, I had to make sure they had either a packed lunch or money for lunch. Of course as a man, I am clothes coordinated challenged. It was a challenge every day to make sure their clothes matched. After all, they were only six and eight years old when this happened. At first, I really enjoyed the novelty of doing their homework with them. I was also watching a neighbor boy that was their friend.

As our strange society goes, when in November my boys were about one month into this situation, their friend, Ben, was about one year into his parents' separation. Between the three of them, I had homework for first, second and third grade. The bus would come home and I would have some kind of snack made for them. Then we would all sit around the table and do homework.

Christmas was strained this year too. Since the boys were born, we always went to my parents' house for Christmas Eve. Since we were the only ones with small children, we always did Christmas day at our house. This was the first year since they were born that they were not with both parents for Christmas. Even when I still worked for the police department, I had earned enough seniority that I could usually get off sometime on Christmas day to spend sometime with them. Even the years I couldn't I would be home for some part of the day.

I continued trying to plan little trips as we could afford them. We tried to do something different or fun every weekend. Truthfully, I'm not sure if I was doing it to keep their minds off what was going on or to keep my mind off it.

My older son, Seth, had had trouble in school since pre-K. My wife and I had had him tested, and everything seemed fine. As he progressed into first and second grade, his problems seemed to get worse. Now he was dealing with the issues of our separation from his mother. I want to say here that I used the phrase "our separation" because in a divorce it isn't just the husband and wife that get divorced, it is the children too.

Because of his problems in school, I asked that the school system re-test him to see is there was some type of special education or programs that would help him. These tests were done at the school in October, November and the beginning of December. The school called us in for a meeting in January to discuss the results of the tests. His mother and I both went to the school and heard the results. They were not really telling me anything I hadn't already noticed. Seth would take a spelling test and get 100% then he would take a vocabulary test and get 100%, and then he would take the comprehension portion for the same story and get 20%. But if you read that same story to him and either forgot as much as one word or switched the order of them he would correct you.

Seth could watch a movie once. If it was a movie he enjoyed, he could almost repeat the movie back to you. He could tell you six months later when a movie was released to the theater. The numbers weren't adding up.

They said that in some areas he scored low enough to qualify for help through special education. However, he scored so high in others; the average was high enough to move him out of what he would have needed to qualify for special education. They also mentioned that Seth expressed concern about our domestic problems. We enrolled him in outside therapy that week.

They also suggested that if I had the time maybe I could volunteer some time in Seth's class. They felt that if I was there it might help his self-confidence and self-esteem. Because I was retired, I was able to go into his class two days a week for an hour each time.

As I assisted in Seth's class, the kids would ask me questions about the things Seth told them we would do. Or they wanted to know what we were doing this weekend since it seemed like we were always doing something. Now a quick note to all of us men. If you wind up in a situation like mine, or if your spouse has the children, be careful what you say to your kids.

One day we were in our little reading group talking about what we wanted to do when we grew up. I guess because Seth had told them I used to be a police officer, usually one would say they wanted to be a police officer. I guess one of them asked if I was still a police officer. I told him no, that was I retired, and tried to explain what that was. One little girl told me her father used to be a doctor. I said oh really, what is he now? She looked me right in the face and with the innocence of a child said, "Oh now he's just crazy." I bet the look on my face was priceless. I quickly changed the subject and moved on.

Seth started seeing his therapist and immediately developed a great rapport with her. The therapist did her best to keep us apprised of these sessions. She started expressing some concern that some of Seth's issues and his statements did not seem to be related to our separation. She asked to see the tests the school had done on him.

She and the school felt Seth was suffering from ADHD. We were advised to take him to our pediatrician and ask him for his input. We took him to see his doctor and based on the school's tests and comments as well as ours, the doctor agreed Seth was ADHD and he was started on medication.

As he continued with his therapy, the therapist told us she felt Seth might need further, more in depth testing. She thought there might be more than the expected trauma of the separation going on. She suggested we have him tested at the Kennedy Kreiger Institute in Baltimore.

If you are not familiar with that institution, it is arguably the world's finest institution dealing with any type of brain disorders. They specialize in brain disorders in children. Our therapist told us she felt Seth was displaying symptoms of autism, more specifically Asperger's syndrome. She suggested he be tested for it. I called the institute and was put on the waiting list.

In late April of 2004, the boy's mother moved from Maryland to Indianapolis, moving in with her cousin. In early May, in the evening one Monday night, the institute called and said, they had a last minute cancellation and could I bring Seth in tomorrow. Of course, we took the appointment.

The testing took place on two consecutive Tuesdays. Both days were all day testing. These tests ranged from story telling to questionnaires of his family history. Seth had to repeat numbers and stories. He was given a physical examination. At the end of both days the doctor called me in and told me, they believed Seth was suffering from Asperger's syndrome. Asperger's is considered a high functioning form of autism. Both doctors concurred that he was ADHD and they felt he had a minor neuromotor dysfunction. I was given information to read on all of these disorders and sent home.

By the time, I received the official written transcripts of their diagnosis the school year was almost over. The boys went to Indianapolis to spend a week with their mother, and I prepared for our summer camping trip, back to Ocean City.

The boys and I, and the family dog, along with their friend Ben, went to a campground just outside of Ocean City called Frontier Town. We arrived on July 1 for a month long camping trip. We set up the camper and went swimming. We spent the forth of July in the campground. We watched the fireworks in Ocean City from the little marina at the campground.

Part of the appeal of Frontier Town is their Old West-themed park. The boys can ride horses, a stagecoach, and an old steam train. Of course, the train ride and the stagecoach ride involve being robbed of the gold shipment. They have staged shoot-outs and a re-enactment of the gunfight at the OK Corral. That one is especially nice because after the shoot out, they pick little kids to play both sides and have their own re-enactment of the shoot out. Over the course of two visits, all three boys were chosen as deputies and given a ceremonial shave at the barbershop. They all also were able to take part in the shoot-out at the OK Corral.

Ben's mother and sister came down the next week to take him home. Over the next month, we had visits from my parents, my daughter, and another family from the street we live on. They brought their two children.

When my parents visited, my father and I took the boys fishing. Now I must tell you about my father and fishing. He is one of those people that when he goes fishing, the fish fight to get on his hook. Between the four of us fishing for about two hours, Seth caught one flounder that was it.

Undaunted, the next day we went back to the same area. This time we didn't bring fishing rods, we brought a seine net. Two people handle this type of net. Weights on one side of the net keep it against the ground, and floats keep the other side at the surface. We soon found out why we didn't catch any fish the day before. Blue crabs had come into the cove we were fishing in and were sloughing their shells. During the first few hours after they shed the old, hard shell, the crab's shell is softer than human skin. The crabs turn from predatory scavengers to every fish's delight.

Right before it finally sloughs off the old hard shell, it splits open at the back; this is called a peeler. We kept one of the peelers and took it back to the campsite. I put it into a cooler of water, by itself to continue the processes of sloughing the hard shell. After it did, I called the boys over to see it. The new soft crab was at least twice as big as his old hard shell was. It was so much bigger that the only way I could prove it to Spencer that is was the same crab and not two different crabs was to let him pick up the old hard crab and see the shell was empty.

Now soft crab sandwiches are considered a delicacy not only for the fish. I could see in my mother's eyes that she was sizing that brand new soft crab up for a hard roll, some lettuce a little mayonnaise and a few slices of tomato. Seth however would have no part of it. He and I took the crab it back, and let it go.

Every year we get a permit and drive onto the beach, at Assateague Island National Park. This is one of those beaches where you let the air out of the tires, drive right onto the beach, and back your truck up to the surf. Because it is not as crowded as the commercial public beaches in Ocean City, the boys get an opportunity to see and do things they otherwise would not be able to see or do. We went swimming, flew kites buried each other in the sand, built sandcastles and watched the dolphins.

One time we watched people on surfboards surfing and others, para sailing. The boys watched some men surf fishing catch a stingray. Seth was especially glad to see the men release it back into the surf. Once, a jellyfish washed up onto the shore right where the boys had been playing only minutes before. This jellyfish was so big that even some of the surf fishermen came over to look at it.

The real draw to Assateague Island is the wild ponies and deer that live on the island. We used to drive there at dusk, by then the day-trippers would be gone and the deer would be out. They seemed to know they were in a protected area because they showed no fear of the cars, or of us

This was my first real time as a single parent. I didn't know how I would feel doing things like leaving the boys when I had to take the dog for a walk. During the day, I let them do it. Those middle of the night walks were different. You have to walk the dog long enough so you aren't walking her again in another hour. I worried though about the boys waking up and me not being there. They have had and are still having some issues with that topic. I am told that it is normal for children to assume if one parent leaves, the other may too.

I had to figure out how I was going to wash clothes without dragging the boys to the Laundromat for the day. Fortunately, at Frontier Town the Laundromat is located near the front pool. I would get the boys settled in at the pool, and put the clothes in the washing machine. In-between washing and drying, I went back to the pool to check on them. The layout of this pool and Laundromat is such that the boys couldn't leave without walking past me. This added to the fact that the front pool consisted of the kiddy pool that was a maximum of about eighteen inches deep and a lazy river ride. Both of the boys can swim and failing that, I guess they could always stand up.

We left in the beginning of August and I brought the boy's home. They left for a two-week stay with their mother. While they were visiting with their mother, I took the written reports I had received from Kennedy Krieger to the school. I spoke briefly with the school's principal. She said we would be having another meeting with Seth's teachers again like last year. They would use the diagnosis from the institute to set up any special classes he would need.

They came home for about a week and the new school year started. Seth was going into forth grade and Spencer, my younger son, was going into second. This would be my first full school year of trying this on my own. Ben's mother had remarried over the summer and he had moved and would be attending another school. In a way, I was glad that I would only be responsible for my two.

CHAPTER TWO: SOCIETY'S VIEWS

Let's first look at the views our society has toward men and women in general. There was a commercial for a popular mid-sized truck. In this commercial, a man is coming home with a small make-up table in the bed of the truck. He stops at a stop sign and sees a motorcycle for sale. When he gets home, he is met by his wife, who sees the motorcycle in the bed of the pick-up. She looks as if she is furious, until he opens one of the four doors and there in the back passenger compartment is her make-up table. She looks at him and punches him in the stomach.

Another commercial featured a husband and wife in their home. The husband did something the wife wasn't happy with. Her response was to promptly slap him in the back of his head.

I have to wonder if these commercials would have been so well received or even aired if the man had hit the woman, of course it wouldn't have. You can't hit or portray violence against women. Yet it happened frequently against men. Our society says it is funny when a man is hit by a woman.

The latest in this vein starts with a young boy on an ice hockey rink. He is alone except for an adult in the goal, in full goalie pads. The child starts to take shot after shot at the goal. The adult fights valiantly to block the shots. At the end, the child shows a few sniffles. The adult takes off their facemask to reveal it is a woman. The voice over narrator extols the virtues of the brand of tissue, and mothers.

How many commercials have we all seen for any number of products, being advertised by any number of sports figures, and what do they all invariably look at the camera and say, "Hi, Mom."

TV commercials as well as movies have been made based solely on the chaos that inevitably results from leaving a man alone at home, with his children. Clearly, we believe men just incapable of taking care of himself much less a family. Even in movies with just single men and women. The woman's house or apartment is always spotless. The man's place on the other hand has wall-to-wall dirty clothes and is decorated in old pizza delivery boxes.

One of the most recent commercials involving interactions between a male parent and a child is that of a young teen girl and her father. She asks him for eighty dollars for a pair of jeans. "Do all of your friends have them?" Everybody has them she tells him. He then asks her if they are designer jeans. She says yes and he asks the name of the designer. Is he a caring, loving father that takes his daughter to the store to get her jeans? Does he give her the money to go buy them herself? No, he goes to his laptop and places a buy order through his online brokerage firm. She does, at the end, remind her father, and he does give her the money.

Today's single parent is increasingly breaking what society as a whole thinks of when they think of a single parent. Most think of an unwed mother struggling to make ends meet. A deadbeat dad off somewhere is living their life as they wish. Never paying child support or paying it erratically enough that it provides little or no real help.

Recently I was at the Red Cross giving blood. The woman there and I started talking about our children. After I told her I was raising my boys by myself she told me she was dating a man doing the same. She told me he was raising three children on his own. She told me how her girlfriends had told her she shouldn't date him because taking on the responsibility of three kids was too much. I have to wonder if that same group of well meaning women were in a restaurant and overheard a group of men advising their friend to stay away from a woman because she had kids, would they have agreed with them, or more likely they would have been incensed by these callous, heartless men.

Another view of a single parent that would come to mind is that of the wronged wife. A long-suffering wife and/or mother abandoned by her cad of a husband. Continuing the stereotype further would have him leaving for a younger woman.

There is also the widow or widower, as I mentioned my friend earlier. While these cases are all different, and within these different situations, everyone is different, there is one common thread. More and more single parents are being left to raise their children by themselves. And increasingly these singles are men.

As I found myself starting the process of raising my children as a single male parent I found some interesting things. I was surprised to find more fathers raising their children than I thought I ever would. Again, it matters not how we found ourselves in this straight, the fact is here we are and now what?

It hadn't dawned on me the difference of opinion between a single male and a single female parent until my neighbor said something to me. She mentioned that the women at church were talking about my situation. Everyone said it was a shame, but that was about it. My neighbor said how she remembers similar conversations with these same women about single female parents, offers of fixing a dinner every now and then, watching the children so she could "have a little time to herself." Helping her clean the house once real good. But in my case, "he's a strong man, he can handle it," were common comments.

It was odd my neighbor would say something; because it was in church, I felt the most out of place. There was any number of women and their children with no male figure around in church. I was the only man, by himself with no wife around with children. The next time you are in your own church, look around for yourself.

I began to pay close attention to what and how people talked to me, and to the female single parents I know. Most of the females were comforted with comments like, "I can't believe he left you and the kids," or "Is he seeing another woman?" or "How could he do this to you?"

I however was greeted and comforted with statements like, "You're an adult; if she wanted to leave you that's between you and her. I can't believe she did this to the boys," or "How are the boys taking it?" I even heard, "Lots of women leave their husbands and I can understand that, but I could never leave my kids." The feelings seemed to me to be split along gender lines. Not by the person saying it, but by the gender of the spouse left to raise the children.

I think personally the harshest thing I have had said to me is when people, mostly women, say I can understand her leaving you, but how could she leave her kids. Now before you start thinking I am some guy just feeling sorry for himself, think about this. I'm sure everyone knows a woman that is a single parent. Think how you would feel walking up to her and saying, I can understand him leaving you, but how could he leave the kids? No one would ever think of saying that to a woman, but men get it all the time.

The more I started to hear comments like these, and the more I thought about them I wasn't sure how I should take them. When people say things like how could a mother leave her children, what are they really saying? Are they saying they expect and even accept when men leaves their children? Are men really that unreliable of parents that people don't even bat an eye when men leave their families behind? When I hear someone say what a good job I am doing with the boys, is what they really are saying is that I am doing a good job, well for a man?

In my generation, there have been great strides in women's rights. There is much more needed, but as women achieve more power in the workplace, in elected office, they have gotten I feel, a little bigger bite of the apple than they expected. The rate of heart attacks in women has skyrocketed. Welcome to the world of corporate stress. Again as I stated in the preface I in no means am attempting to "bash" anyone, just stating societal values that are in the process of changing.

Twenty years ago, you never heard of a woman leaving her children and husband behind. As women achieve more equality with men, they have unfortunately picked up our bad habits. Again, looking at it as society does, a man that leaves his wife and children is rarely looked at in a poor light. The most often question asked of him is, "So how much is this going to cost you?" or maybe "How much child support will you have to pay?" When a man leaves, it appears that society boils it down to a financial matter. The family, children, or marriage implications are replaced with a dollar sign.

When a woman leaves, without the children, just the opposite seems to happen. Everything centers on what "she" did to the family unit. What "she" did to the kids. The only time money is brought into it is how they plan to split the marital property. Men leave expecting to have to pay large amounts of child support. Women haven't been exposed to that, yet. This is not fair, or equitable, but it is often true. A man that leaves his family behind is simply thought of as moving on. A woman that does exactly the same thing is often looked at in a much harsher light.

I believe for these reasons we tend to raise our children differently. Every girl "helps" mom do the laundry. They see mom doing the sewing, cooking and cleaning. Boys help dad wash the car. A boy might be invited "under" the car for an oil change. No one would hand their daughter a wrench and invite her to help dad fix the leaky sink.

When I am at the grocery store I have started paying closer attention on how parents, particularly female parents shop with their children. The boys seem to be mostly "in tow" somewhat just along for the ride. The girls however are shown items before they are put in the cart. I have seen girls pick up the wrong loaf of bread. Mom takes it and puts it back explaining to her daughter why we aren't buying that one today. Maybe they have coupon, or another brand is on sale. These are explained and the correct one is picked up. I have seen a boy do the same thing. The loaf of bread is put back, the correct one picked up and not a word is spoken.

Men are by no means innocent of these types of acts. How many men do you know of that would take their daughter to the auto parts store and explain the difference between winter and summer windshield wiper fluid. Boys are the ones who cut the grass with dad, not their daughters. Even in today's society that is begging for equality we as parents continue the stereotypical raising of our children. If this stereotyping was still true and it was for the most part men that left their wives and children, this might be OK. It is however not the stereotype anymore.

Men calm down it will be your turn soon. I take my hat off to all women. As a gender you either are, or seem to be, at least far more qualified to be, and do without us than we without you. When a man walks out on his family except for immediate financial concerns women get along just fine. I unfortunately cannot say the same thing about my fellow man. The vast majority of men are woefully unprepared to face the solo raising of a family. This may be part of the reason men seem to get remarried so quickly after a divorce.

I am not talking about the bachelor that never cleans his house. Or the one that sorts his clothes into dirty, dirty but OK, dirty but OK if I throw it into the dryer and, call the EPA. I am talking about the average man that even if his wife works, she is still responsible for the majority of the day-to-day running of the household.

Men, get over it. This is the year 2007, the odds of you having to protect your family from the marauding saber tooth tiger are slim. You need to help out a little around the house. If you can't get past that macho thing about it being "women's work," then do it for yourself. Do you really want to be helpless again? Your mother probably will get tired real fast of doing your laundry. Your boys will not be any less masculine if they know how to cook or clean. You daughters will not be tomboys if they know how to start the lawn mower and cut the grass.

We as parents need to drag our society kicking and screaming into the reality of single male parenthood. They are a fact, and their numbers are growing. We as parents and society as a whole have done a poor job preparing our male children for that event.

Before we get to the men, I feel it is necessary to mention something here. It doesn't matter how it happens, divorce, death or some other type of separation. Again as our society changes, more men are becoming single parents. As I said earlier, I served as a police officer for twenty-six years. I worked in a suburban area not far from Washington DC. Every year the month of May is National Police Week. There is a week set aside to mark the police officers killed in the line of duty that year. As I attended these events, I was stunned as I noticed an alarming trend.

I defy anyone to watch the widow of a slain police officer holding the hand of her orphaned child walking through the gathered police and not shed a tear, another child that will never know their father. As the years went on not only are more and more police being killed, but I started noticing a single male dressed in a dark suit. This time he is holding the hand of his orphaned child, another child that will never know their mother. Looking back on it, this man lost more than a wife; his children lost their mother, and they both lost a female figure in his child's life.

OK men your turn. It seems in our society a single woman raising her children by herself is a woman with baggage. After all society tells us, many men don't want to raise their own children, why would they want to raise someone else's? A single man raising his children by himself is often looked at in an entirely different light. We are a sensitive caring man. A man that cares enough about his own children to raise them all by himself, he must be a great catch. He could help me raise my children. I hear all the time how great I am with the boys. What a great father I am. I wonder when was the last time a single female mother heard the same compliments. Women are for the most part expected to be good parents. If a man does it, every one is surprised.

Again going back to the stereotypical way a person becomes a single parent. Even in those cases, women are much more considerate than men are. When the time comes for the man to leave, most women help them pack. By the time he gets back to the house, she has graciously packed his belongings and has them waiting at the curb for him.

Men note, if you are making this move on trash day, make sure you get there before the trash man does. You see, your new luggage is most probably either black or white and made of plastic.

Women on the other hand seem to think this through more carefully. They already have in their mind what they intend to take, which usually amounts to half. While it seems like it, I am not trying to bash anyone, just trying to look at things with humor and through society's eye. A woman thinks about taking things like pots and pans. She knows you need things like that to run a household. Not only are they not important to a man, has he never used them. Well except for the time, he used the good five-quart saucepan to catch the water when he was cleaning out the trap in the bathroom sink.

It isn't until you have need for such things that you even realize they are gone. Let me again use myself as the brunt of a funny story. Like most police officers, I have been married more than once. When my first wife left, I left the house, and like most men, I told her to take whatever she wanted. Well she took me at my word. After a few weeks, I looked through the cupboard to see what was left. I saw a can of ravioli. I thought great, supper will be served soon. I looked for a pot to heat it in. That is when I learned I didn't have any pots. I didn't care I could always microwave it. Oops, that was gone too.

Now how much time was I spending in the kitchen to not realize the microwave oven was gone? Who cares, I'm a man I'll eat it cold, right out of the can. That was a great idea, until I noticed the can opener was gone. I hung my head and put my can of ravioli back in the cupboard. This story was so appreciated by my caring male friends that on the one-year anniversary of my divorce, they gave me a can of ravioli, a plastic fork, and a hand operated can opener. I still have the can opener. I received a similar gift from my brother at Christmas.

In this case, society again said this was OK. After all my wife had our daughter to raise, she needed these things more than I did. Could you imagine a man leaving and taking everything? While I'm sure it happens, society just seems to look at it differently.

I agree with, and can understand where some of these beliefs come from. Again, the values and the laws covering divorce were a long time in the making. For too many years, a man could just leave his wife and children. Take all of the family assets and pay little or no child support. The average woman didn't have the level of education or job skills that are available to, and held by many women today. The day of the poor uneducated woman having to enter the steno pool is about over for mainstream America. Most families are two income families. In many, the woman makes comparable or in a few cases more than the man. Of course, there are still disparities, but I think most would agree that society has made great strides toward equality for women.

Along with this, again, I believe, is the empowering notion that "I don't need a man." This is true, but something gets lost in the transition. Men and women alike have to keep in mind, that in a marriage there is more to consider than whether or not you "need" a man or woman in your life. You have an even more important mission now than your marriage; you have a greater responsibility to your children than you have to yourself.

Yes, a man on his income, supporting only himself would probably improve his life stile. And yes, the same could be said about many women. If a woman that was employed leaves her husband and her children supporting only herself, her style of living would probably improve. This however, is also unfortunately true; no matter which way it goes, when one parent is left to raise children. The standard of living of the children, suffers.

CHAPTER THREE: BASIC NEEDS

Enough preaching about society's ills, lets get on with our lives. Most men have no idea of how much it takes to keep a house running. In the movie The Matrix one of the characters mentions that the programs that do their jobs are never noticed. Only the programs that malfunction are noticed. That is the same type of position we men have allowed ourselves to get into. We expect to open the sock drawer and "poof" there are clean socks. We assume sometime during the night the clean clothes fairy came in and gathered up all the dirty clothes, washed, dried, folded them and put them back.

Men, believe it or not, the windows on your house do not get clean every time it rains. Unfortunately the opposite is true, they get dirtier. You really do have to pick up the things on the table or shelve before you dust the table or shelve. I'll explain what dusting is later. While cleaning is important, it is way down the list for the beginner. First things first.

Remember high school psychology? There was a list called Maslow's hierarchy of needs. In case you need a little refresher it goes something like this. First come physiological needs. These are the basic needs to sustain life, food, water, and oxygen.

Next come safety needs. Most of us as adults take this for granted, as the aforementioned saber tooth tiger is no longer with us. However, that does not mean that threats to your safety no longer exist. Children often will display the signs of insecurity and the need to be safe. Remember they have, in their minds, lost a parent. They may have lost the only home they have ever known. To a child you were their protector and provider. You have to first and foremost reassure your children that they are safe and that they are still loved. If you wind up having to move to a different house or even a different town, or state, try to take something along with you that is your little piece of home. Don't let either anger or sorrow let you throw away things your children deserve to see. Pictures of them and their mother, even things like your wedding pictures. These things may be the last thing you want to see right now, but your children should at least have the opportunity to decide for themselves if they want to see them or not. If you destroy them you can't get them back again.

The third level of Maslow's hierarchy is the need for love, affection and to belong to a group or unit. As he continued Maslow went into needs for self-esteem and when all other needs are met, self-actualization. Don't worry, I, like most men get confused around big words too so hold on. We'll get to some of the other needs later, but let's cover a basic, food.

Household chores include a lot more than cleaning. While cleanliness may be next to Godliness, it can wait around the house, again, first things first. Your children and you still need to eat. Don't run out and buy stock at the local fast food store. You will have to venture into the bastion of womanhood, the grocery store. This might be harder than some think. Remember the average husband doesn't do the cooking around the average household. More do, but many still don't, and even fewer still do the grocery shopping. So how do you go to the store and buy groceries if you don't know what you need to buy to make a meal? Before you can start, you first have to swallow something, your male pride. Don't expect to become Emeril Lagasy in two days in the kitchen. Just work on the staples. Your kids will give you some idea of what they like and will eat.

You do not have to become Betty Crocker either though. Remember it doesn't matter how the meal starts. What matters is what it looks like and how it tastes once it gets to the plate. Go to your store's frozen food section. Most stores sell frozen meals or dinners in bags that are almost man proof. Most are designed to be made in one dish, either in the oven or one pan on the stove. In general, frozen meals seem to be a little healthier than dried ones, especially the all in one bag variety. At least on the sodium count, but take a look at the fat content too, it may surprise you.

For those of you not real familiar with a kitchen, the oven is that big opening under the stove top where you keep your pots and pans. Here would be a good place to mention that you will want to remove those pots and pans before you preheat the oven. The plastic handles tend to melt at 350 degrees. Even if you don't have plastic handles they are really hot when you try to take them out of the oven.

Even the adult that works a full-time job can, with today's appliances, prepare a full meal that everybody will like. For example, if you don't have, or don't have any more, a crock-pot, go buy one. If you have to get a new one, look for a larger one, you can always put in less but you can't over fill them. I'm sure when the crock-pot was first introduced, as a slow cooker; men were not given a second thought. The crock-pot can be a savior to a single father, any single parent for that matter. It can prepare almost all of the things you should look for as you think about preparing meals. You can put your meal in and it cooks itself. You really have to try to ruin a meal made in a crock-pot. Crock-pots are not used only for roasts either, chicken, turkey, soups and one of my favorites, spaghetti sauce turn out great. What we will cover here are the basics of a kitchen and shopping for food.

First make your kitchen man friendly. Remember the hardest thing you may have cooked in the past was heating up a bowl of dried noodles by adding boiling water. Let's take a look what appliances you have to work with. Which ones you had better never touch, and what you may need to try to get. I made a joke before about the stove and oven. I have pre-heated the oven without first checking inside to make sure it was indeed empty. An oven or stove usually consists of two very different heating areas, the top or stove, and the oven. I know this may seem a bit simplistic, but bare with me.

The stove top usually has four burners. They are used for frying or boiling. This is where you use pots and frying pans. Everyone knows this, we hope. Here is what a lot of men don't know, and trust me this is a recipe for disaster. It doesn't matter what type of burner you have, when you turn if off it stays HOT. For anyone having trouble following this let me put it this way.

When you put your car in park and turn off the engine, you do not expect it to continue driving three or four more blocks without you. Well this is just what your burner does. If you turn off a burner, leave a pot sitting on it, and walk away, whatever is in it, will burn. Gas stove tops are not as bad with this as electric, but there is an even greater danger than burning your food.

Remember the car example? You would not think twice about putting your car in park and turning it off walking in front, or in back of it, to get into your home or work. Of course not, once you turn off your car it is off. Unlike your car, the burner on your stove is still extremely hot. If you try to wipe up a spill, or even worse touch the surface with your bare hand, you will be badly burned. This will be even worse if one of your children touches it.

Also unlike your car, a stove top burner can be on a little bit. Your car is either on or it is off. Not so with your stove top. Burners can be turned down so low that they appear off. If you want your burner off, make sure it is turned all the way off. You don't want to be like me by smelling the burner the next morning when you get up to fix breakfast.

The other part of this appliance is the oven. This is the big box looking thing you bake cakes in. This is also where you would bake chicken, turkeys, or any of your baked goods like cakes or cookies. The biggest hurtle here is remembering what you are dealing with. Let's go back to the car for a moment.

If you wanted to work on you car's motor you would of course wait until it was cool enough to touch. Or you might work on it the first thing in the morning when it was still cool. Again your oven is just the opposite. Here is an appliance that you heat up to several hundred degrees, then open it and stick in your hand. Most of the time, your face will also come uncomfortably close to going into the oven.

Then after you put a piece of metal or glass in the oven, heat it, and its contents to several hundred degrees, you put your hand back into the oven and remove this hot piece of metal or glass.

Let me plug a safety feature that every kitchen needs, and too few have. There is a small bracket that needs to be attached to the floor and to the back frame of your oven. If you are not sure if you have one or not, do this. With both the oven and stove turned off and cool. Make sure there are no children around. Open the oven door. Put your hand or foot on the door and push down, gently. If this bracket is not installed it will amaze you how easily the entire appliance will flip over. You can imagine if one of your children or you for that matter did this while the stove had something boiling on it. Or if the oven was hot. If your oven does not have this feature, put down this book and get it installed. I'll wait.

Another extremely man friendly appliance I have found is a counter top grill marketed by a famous ex-boxer. You don't need to buy his, everybody else's work just fine too. They heat up themselves, have timers, and are relatively easy to clean. They even leave little grill marks on your food. You will find which ones you like and which ones you don't. Here is a quick clean up tip on this one. As soon as you are done cooking and take the food off the grill, unplug it and lay a few wet paper towels in it and re-close it. This acts kind of like a steam cleaner and will really simplify the clean up.

I mentioned the unfortunate loss of my microwave. This appliance must have been made with men in mind. Push a button and the door opens. Place the food you want to cook inside and push the door closed. Now here comes the real man friendly feature, look at the front of the microwave oven. You will most likely see a picture of what you want to cook. Push the picture and the microwave oven will come on. Most even have a built in turntable that rotates your meal as it cooks.

Another safety note for the microwave challenged man. Your

microwave oven has just taken your potpie from frozen hard as a rock, to bubbly in a matter of minutes. Well guess what? Not only did it heat your food, it heated everything else. Whatever you set your potpie on is just as hot. I might also mention a few things that really shouldn't go in a microwave oven. For the most part you want to stay away from putting metal, plastic or Styrofoam in your microwave.

Along the lines of the microwave oven is the toaster oven. I can also vouch for the versatility of the lowly toaster oven. You have to have some type of toaster. You will never get through breakfast without one. Get a toaster oven that can do double duty. Look for one that has a broiler and bake feature. You probably will not be broiling your sirloin under it, but your kids will flip over how well it makes hot-dogs.

Tabletop grills, microwave ovens, and toaster ovens, great as they are can't do everything. I know you may not want to think about it but you will have to eventually cook something. For this you need a good set of man friendly pots and pans. For the novice in the kitchen I strongly recommend pots and pans with a non-stick surface. If you are buying them for the first time, here is a pretty good rule of thumb to go by. While size may or may not matter, weight does. For the most part, if you choose a set of fairly heavy, non-stick pots and pans, you will be pleased with the results. You might even want to look at getting a large non-stick wok; they are easy to use and clean. They work great with the all in one bag-frozen meals.

Another man friendly tip, saying non-stick is like saying waterproof. If you look closely at anything listed as waterproof you will normally see a depth limit, or see that the more correct description of the item should be water-resistant. Non-stick pots and pans are really not non-stick, they are stick resistant. Trust me, if something can stick or burn on, you can, with enough effort make it stick or burn.

Care must be used when cleaning your non-stick pots and pans. Now I know how tempting it is to break out the steel wool pad and clean that bad boy right up. You are not cleaning the wheels on your car. You can and you will clean the non-stick finish right off of your new cookware.

Should you have great-grand mom's cast iron skillet, it along with all other cast iron cookware have unique cleaning needs. If you wash them with nice hot soapy water, you will wash off the "seasoning" that makes it work so well. One of the best ways to clean them is with hot water and sea salt. This will clean it with out washing the seasoning out of the cookware.

My daughter gave me for Christmas one year a pizza cooker. This is also one of the most man friendly kitchen appliances. This pizza cooker consists of a round cooking pan on which you place the frozen pizza and a double-armed cooker. The pan rotates in between the two horizontal cooking arms. This unit can be set to cook from the top, the bottom, or both. It comes with a timer that turns off the unit. What is really nice about this unit is that as the pan rotates through these arms you can add toppings. This means you can buy basic stripped cheese pizzas and turn them into any fancy topped pizzas you want. If you shop your grocery store wisely, there is always some kind of pizza on sale. I frequently find cheese or pepperoni pizzas for fewer than two dollars each. With the features on this type of cooker, you can put on any toppings you please as you are cooking it. It is also quite easy to clean.

The last kitchen gadget I can personally recommend is one of the vacuum food sealers. Leftovers are going to become your friend. Plus there are any number of things you can seal with them, not just the bags they provide. If you are like me and your children are like mine, you will soon find you are rotating two to four different bags of breakfast cereals. With these sealers, you can reseal the cereal bags and keep the cereal fresh. This goes for bags of potato chips, cheese curls or any number of snack foods you keep around the house. If you decide to buy one of these units, you will get many suggestions on how to freeze fresh fruits or vegetables when they are cheaper in season.

Other things like non-stick electric griddles and waffle irons will come, but for right now, they are just something else to find a place to store when you are not using it. I hate to sound like an infomercial but one thing they say is true. No matter how handy a small appliance is, if it is out of sight, you probably will not use it.

I have tried using food processors. I think they should be banned from every kitchen in America. Especially from any household with only one parent. This ban should remain in effect until the manufacturer agrees to send a factory representative with it. Not only to use it for you but clean it once they are done using it. If you feel it is necessary to get a blender, consider one of those hand held stick blenders. They will remind you of one of those things you should use to mix a can of paint. For most blending needs they work just as well, and cleaning them is great.

Unless you are already familiar with a hand held mixer, you may want to stay away from them. I know the best part of using them was licking the batter off the beaters before your mother washed them, but they have the potential of being very messy.

If your children are in school and you work, breakfast will have to be catch as catch can, but try to provide something. If money permits, most public schools have a breakfast program just like the lunch program we all know and love. If funds don't permit, you will have to stay with something relatively simple. Maybe even get it ready the night before. Pour the cereal into the bowl and cover it with plastic wrap for the next morning. Then in the morning, you or your kids can just add milk and go.

This might also be a good place to bring up school lunches. I am raising two boys. If both of my boys bought a school lunch every day of the week, for a month it would come to eighty dollars a month just in school lunches. You will have to learn how to make and pack a school lunch. Again, this is where you get to teach the kids how to shop while learning what to buy. Of course, as a parent, you want some type of well-balanced meal for your children, usually a sandwich, a treat, and a drink. The sandwich and drink part are, for the most part, pretty straightforward. It is the snack that can get tricky. Giving a child an orange might sound like a wonderful idea, lots of vitamin C, and all. Have you ever eaten an orange and not gotten the juice all over yourself? How about the little pieces of orange rind that will be under your fingernails for the rest of the day? Fortunately, there are healthy snacks that you children will like. They will be shaped like their favorite cartoon character or some other strange shape or flavor. If you want to stay with fruit, there are fruit bowls you can send in with them.

I have found juice boxes are a great help too. Most schools will not allow glass containers into the school. The juice bags may be a different story. You will have to base their use on your knowledge and the age of your children. Too many times have I seen this. A child holds the juice bag firmly in one hand, read firmly as squeezing. Then with the other hand, they are supposed to punch a plastic straw through a small pre-marked hole. If you are lucky, they will only miss the hole and bend the straw. If your luck holds like mine, the straw will punch right through the bag, first try. However remember the hold firmly, squeeze I mentioned a little while back? Lets just say, think Mount St. Helen's of sticky sugary fruit juice spraying all over your child, halfway through the school day.

Again, on the subject of asking for what you are entitled to, most schools offer some type of reduced priced lunches and some type of breakfasts. If you are raising your kids by your self, swallow your male pride and ask for things that may help your kids.

Supper or dinner depending on what part of the country you live in may be the most important meal of the day. Even if it isn't very fancy, it provides something at least as, if not more important that the meal itself. It provides you and your children an opportunity to sit down as a family. If there is a TV in the room, turn it off. I moved the kitchen table to the other side of the house to get us away from the TV. It doesn't matter what you talk about, school, homework, their friends, just make sure you talk with and about them and your family.

Now if you're not used to having supper as a family, or maybe your work schedule prohibits it most nights, let me suggest an icebreaker. Every now and then, maybe once a week fix spaghetti for your family. Then have everybody put on a clean white t-shirt. The goal of this meal is to see who can go the longest without getting any spaghetti sauce on their shirt. We'll get into laundry later.

Another area the average man will need help with is keeping your children in social groups. Looking again back at Maslow's needs, after basic needs like food and shelter are met, he says that we then enter the area where we need love, affection and belongingness. In our society, most of the groups that the average man belongs to are associated with adult activities. Sporting events, hobbies like hunting, sport boating and quite frankly having a few with your friends after work or while watching that big game.

You may try to include your younger children in your at home party during the big game. And some of your children may even feign some amount of interest; after all, all men like sports right? Maybe not, maybe your children only watch it so they can spend time with you. My two boys are night and day. They are clearly brothers, I feel for the person that picks on one of them, because I can see the "if you mess with my brother, you mess with me" logic already forming.

Most children get their group affiliations through school or sports. Spencer is too young to start being involved with the youth group at our church. Seth is old enough to start this year. It is your job as a parent to make sure your children have a good fit. Looking at my brother and me as we were growing up, my older brother seemed to love going to school. He studied and read all the time. I can remember at one time it seemed to me that he knew every fact about World War I. I never liked school. I wasn't that bad of a student, I just didn't like it.

As manly as you think, it might make you to have your boys playing every sport you can get them into. As much or as little effort they seem to put into the sport, they may only be doing it to please you. If you put your children in sports, the band, the chess club, or no school activities at all, choose them based on the children's wants and needs, not on yours.

I don't want this to turn into a religious tirade, but I feel the church can be a very important part of both your and your children's lives. You and your children have experienced a trauma only matched by death, you maybe have. If you have found yourself raising your children by your self through death, I offer my most heart felt sympathy.

I have been told by more than one therapist that in a divorce it is often harder for both you and the children. In death, there is closure. No one left you or the children by choice; they were taken from you in death. In a divorce, there will always be the question of why hanging over your and your children's minds.

In your children's need to belong, the one unit that they should always be a part of, their family has been broken. I think you need to try to keep things as close to normal as possible. When I say normal, I mean normal to the children. If you used to go to church, continue going. Shop at the same stores; go on vacation like you used to do. I understand that in most times where there is a single parent money is an issue, but within reason try to keep thing the same.

In most relationships it appears that, the male half, the father, is somewhat reactionary. They come home from work and then react to whatever happened with their family that day. As a single parent, you no longer have that luxury. Here is something that is a novel idea, ask your kids what they want to do. One night at supper, Spencer, my youngest started talking about skiing and snow boarding. We talked about that for a while then he mentioned ice-skating. We talked about that for a while I asked him if he wanted to take lessons. He said no and dropped the topic.

I had to remind myself that I had another child to think about. Seth is not Spencer, what interests Spencer may not interest Seth. While Spencer wants to play outside and ride his bike, Seth likes to play by himself, taking apart and putting back together his toys. Since Spencer was able to ask questions and talk about something he wanted to do, I had to make sure Seth felt included. I asked him if he wanted to try any of the things we had talked about. He just said no. I remembered he had talked about something he wanted to do. So I asked him if he wanted to build a robot. Seth brightened up; knowing this was something he wanted to do.

Of course, I'm not really sure how we plan on building a robot. But since he said he wanted to do it, and I asked him about it, I at least have to make an effort. We found a book that included a kit to make a model of one of the Mars Rovers. I asked him if he wanted to get it and we could build it. I think he thinks robots should be more human looking, so he passed on the offer. But at least there was an offer made to include him in activity he wants to do.

As another example of how your children watch what you as single parent do and how you treat your other children. When I had to take Seth for his testing, the Kennedy Krieger Institute is in Baltimore City. I tried to make a field trip of it instead of making it a day full of testing with a doctor. I told Seth we were going into Baltimore City. He enjoyed seeing the tall buildings and the traffic. Next to the Institute, there was an active construction site. I tried to explain to him the different cranes and derricks working the site. There were bulldozers, large dump trucks, and cement trucks coming and going. It was every little boy's dream. It was kind of fun for the big boy to watch too.

I didn't give to much thought to the fact that we went into the city until several months later. Spencer started asking me if I would take him to Baltimore City. I told him that of course I would. In my mind, I was planning trips to the National Aquarium or the Science center.

One morning Spencer woke up about five thirty and got into bed with me. Normally I would put him back into his, but it was almost time to get up anyway. At six o'clock the alarm went off, I turned off the alarm and turned on the news. Spencer watched it with me. The morning news I watch is of course broadcast from Baltimore City. After each commercial break, they show pictures of the skyline of Baltimore. Spencer asked again if I would take him to Baltimore City. Again, I said we would go and suggested some places we might go. He looked at me and said no daddy I want you to take "me" to Baltimore City. You already took Seth; we should leave him here. It took me back at first, so I asked him if we didn't take Seth who would he stay with. He thought about it for a minute. I assumed that after he thought about it he would want to include his big brother. Instead, he told me we should leave him here that he could stay with Amy.

My adult logic found it hard to believe he would want to exclude his brother from something like a trip to Baltimore City. It wasn't until I stopped looking at it like an adult and father and started looking at it like a brother did it make any sense. I have two brothers; we are each five years apart with me being the middle child. I love my brothers dearly and would do anything to help them. I have always wished the very best for my brothers. But don't all children think their parents love their other siblings more than they do them? In many family relationships this can be somewhat offset by the attentions of the other parent. Raising children as a single parent takes away that option. Even if your spouse lives close by and makes every effort to stay in your children's lives, you are, the one they see interact with them every day. Spencer didn't want anything taken away from Seth; he just wanted what in his mind Seth had already been given.

CHAPTER FOUR: CLEANLINESS IS NEXT TO GODLINESS

I'm sure everyone has been waiting for this chapter. We all probably remember a popular comedian that in his routine talked about men cleaning a house with a leaf blower. While this is funny, in my past profession, I have seen a few houses that could use a good cleaning by this method. I, as well as most police officers can tell you the story of going to a house for a breaking and entering. You get there and look around the house. There are clothes all over the place. The TV is knocked over onto the floor. Then you say something like, I'm really sorry they really trashed your house. Only to have the homeowner say something like, oh they weren't in here; they were only in the bedroom. You have to remember to remove your foot from your mouth before you try to follow them to the room in question.

Remember back in the first chapter where we discussed the differing views of the single male versus the single female parent? Well here is another one, but this one goes in the men's favor. For some reason women are supposed to know how to keep a house clean and men don't. It may not be fair or right, but it is often true. So men take this one.

Now I am going to bring up a topic that all or at least many single parents will understand and agree with. Most dual parent families may not agree, but again in the single parent household certain exceptions must be made. There is a difference between a dirty house and a cluttered house. I'm going out on a limb here, but here goes. If you have been tasked with raising your children by your self, worry about clean first and let clutter, take care of itself. Your children need clean clothes to go to school in. But if they get those clean clothes from the laundry basket, after you have washed them, instead of their dresser, what's the difference? Clean is clean.

Now before I get into specifics of how I do it and some of the time saving tips I have found I have to mention something. As I said there is clean and dirty and there is clutter and straight. A clean house that is cluttered will look dirty. And a not so clean house that is tidy and straight looks clean. It is nice to have a clean and tidy house, but we don't live in a perfect world. If you and your kids learn, just to pick up things you are a long way to a nice looking house.

Go to your local craft store and buy some large wicker baskets. I have them all over my house. One for shoes, one for book bags after school, for blankets, even one for toys in the family room. If they are in the basket, there you go, neat, tidy, clean looking house. While in the craft store, you might want to take a look for some wall hangers for you and your kids, the ones with pegs on them. They come with sports themes or whatever your kids might be interested in. They are great for hanging clothes on instead of throwing them on the floor.

Since I have started with laundry, let's give the man, crash course on washing clothes. Your washer can be your friend. We have evolved from the days of carrying the clothes down to the riverside and pounding them clean with a rock. I never really understood how that worked anyway. Most new washers have several settings. Some are for the size of the load, some for the length of the wash and or rinse cycle; others let you choose regular, permanent press or delicate clothes and the temperature of the water.

Let me address the first one I mentioned the choice of the size of the load. It is a good thing to select the appropriate size load. This saves water, laundry detergent, and therefore money. However, as I found out the hard way, make sure you check it before every load. I once set mine on the small setting and washed a few items of clothes. Then I washed a very full load of towels. I resumed washing clothes as soon as the repairman replaced the burned out bearings in my washing machine.

Again, I will have to go against traditional wisdom. While you are getting familiar with doing the wash you might want to do smaller loads every day, until you get used to doing all the laundry. If you don't, it might be too late when the kids, or you for that matter, are getting ready for school or work and there are no clean clothes in the house.

To continue with laundry 101 you will want to sort your clothes before you wash them. For sake of simplicity, I suggest the following. Darks, this would be blue jeans, dark shirts, dark dress pants, and the like. You will want to wash and rinse these in cold water. Next, I separate out the colored clothes. This includes just about the rest of your clothes.

I used to just sort into colors, whites and towels. One day I had sorted my clothes and noticed that between my two boys and me we almost had enough red clothes to do a load of just red clothes. That is when I started sorting out the darks, from the colors.

During this sorting, is when you should do two very important things. This is when you should apply any type of pre-wash. This normally comes in a spray bottle. I have my suspicions that it is really just liquid detergent in a different package. The other thing you should do is check the pockets. Pants pockets, shirt pockets anything that has pockets. If you are raising boys, you may want to shake things out that don't have pockets.

There is a twofold purpose behind doing this. First, as washer of the clothes, you get to keep all the money or other contraband you may find. While this may be more rewarding, the second is more important. You would be surprised what a mess one piece of paper can make in your washer. Think of machine assisted spitballs.

Oh, but would that be the worst thing that could happen. Wait until the first time you wash an ink pen. Worse yet wash a crayon and don't catch it before you dry that load. If you miss a crayon there are two way to lose. First, if it is in a load of white that you have washed in hot water it will melt all over the rest of the clothes. If it is in the dark or colored clothes you just finished washing in cold water, you will ship it off to the dryer were it can cause some real damage.

If this sounds like the voice of experience speaking again, you're right. I had a crayon melt all over not only the clothes in the dryer, but all over the dryer itself. I have read that a common lubricant like WD40, a credit card, a blow dryer, and a lot of towels help. Oh, I forgot, I am a single male parent, so unless you are raising a girl or two, or stayed in the seventies, you may not have the blow dryer. If this happens to you, good luck.

Enough personal horror stories back to the wash. Choose the proper load size and water temperature for the amount and type of clothes you want to wash. Then turn the water on and start drawing water into the washer.

White clothes should be separated by themselves they should be washed in hot water, rinsing can be done in cold. You may want to use bleach in your white clothes. You may especially may want to add bleach if you have played the spaghetti for dinner game. If you do, there are two ways of safely adding it to the wash. One way is to let the washer fill with water and then start the washer. Before you start adding clothes, add the bleach, before you add the clothes. Actually, that isn't bad advice for every load. After you add the detergent, either bleach alternative or bleach, then add the clothes. Most new machines have an automatic bleach dispenser you can add the bleach to. Now when adding bleach, if you spill any on your hands or on the washing machine, wash your hands with soap and water or use a piece of clothing that is already wet and white. It is not recommended that you wipe you hands off on the blue T-shirt you are wearing.

The next load you need to know about is towels. Bath towels, hand towels or tea towels it doesn't matter. Oh in case you didn't know, a tea towel is that little towel that looks just like the hand towel in the bathroom, except this one you use in the kitchen.

I remember a commercial for a popular fabric softener where a bear dropped a bottle of his fabric softener onto a big stack of nice fluffy bath towels. They looked so nice and soft and fluffy, I wanted to run right out side and roll in the dirt just so I could take a shower and dry off with one of them. I bought a bottle of this fabric softener. I opened it and it smelled as nice and fresh as the commercial promised it would. So I added it to my wash, all of my wash. My boy's blue jeans and mine came out soft and fluffy. The undershirts smelled better than when I bought them.

This was a good thing because I thought I would have to go out and buy all new bath towels. I had fairly new bath towels. They were indeed as soft, fragrant, and fluffy as my spokes-bear told me they would be. They just didn't seem to be drying us off. I was getting dryer from the friction of rubbing the towel against my skin, as I was from the towel absorbing the water. I noticed this with the boy's towels too. Sometimes it almost felt like my skin was almost oily after a shower and drying off on my nice fluffy, fragrant towels. I discussed my dilemma with my mother when I asked her to help me keep a look out for a white sale.

Of course, I didn't want white towels; that is what it is called when things like that go on sale. Who knew? Well guess what? You should carefully watch the amount of fabric softener you use in the wash when you are washing towels. Apparently, the very substance that causes the fluffy fragrant softness I wanted inhibits the absorption of water.

Now I sometimes go into one further separation. If I have enough for a load of wash clothes and towels from the kitchen, I will sometimes wash them by themselves. I add a little bleach to the water. I just like knowing that the things I just used to wipe up or wash up food was cleaned with bleach. Again, men, take the gimme. Yes these wash clothes will fade, or bleach out, but remember we are men, we don't know how to wash clothes. The whole world expects us to wash at least one or two red items with our whites. Now you might expect that if you wash fifteen white undershirts, fifteen pair of white socks and assorted white underwear with one red shirt in hot water and bleach, the shirt would bleach out and turn white. Well you are half-right, the red shirt will be a lighter shade of red, so will all of your other "whites." Since the show Miami Vice has been off the air quite a while, don't send your children to school in pink clothing.

One more handy tip before we move on. If you can remember to check a heavily stained piece of clothing before you dry it, that's a good thing. If you catch it, try re-washing it. If you don't and dry it first, the stain will "set." Either hope the stain is somewhere where no one will see it. If that was true how did you get the stain there in the first place? Or you can always wash and wax the family car one more time.

I know we have spent a lot of time on this one topic, but this is such a visible display of your housekeeping skills that I think it warrants it, anyway I am almost done.

Drying clothes is pretty straightforward. There are a few things to remember. Your dryer will have settings similar to those on your washer. Use the one that best describes the type of clothes you are putting in it. You may also have a setting for the degree of heat you want. For the most part use the coolest setting that will get the clothes dry. This helps cut down on wrinkling. Your dryer can also be used for a cheap dry cleaning alternative. There are kits you can buy that use the heat from your dryer to activate a special cloth. You place the clothes and this special cloth in a special bag. You turn on the dryer for the specified time and there you go home dry cleaned clothes. This works nice for a quick freshen up, cigarette smoke, things like that. But for stains, bite the bullet and take them out.

The other big laundry issue is ironing. I hate ironing. It seems like you can never get the creases to match up. Or if your iron one side of a shirt sleeve smooth, you have ironed a crease into the other side. And of course it is never on the seam, now you have two creases on your sleeve. Things are much easier with the advent of permanent press clothes, which by the way are not. They just seem to be a little less wrinkle prone. The best way to deal with wrinkles is to avoid them in the first place. You can help this process in a number of ways. The bear's fabric softener helps; dryer sheets that smell just like the bear's softener seem to help too. Try not to over dry your clothes. Make sure they are dry; not damp when you take them out of the dryer, but not over dry. Try not to let clothes sit in the dryer. I am terrible about that one.

If that you fall into any of these you can still try one more trick. Take a damp towel, a clean one not the one you just used to dry off with after your shower, and throw it in the dryer. Run it for a few minutes then take your clothes out right away.

Another thing to remember is that the best way to hang pants is on the type of hanger with the little clips on them. Clip the pants by the cuff and gravity will help pull the wrinkles out.

So to recap, sort clothes by color and type. Check them before you wash them and before you dry them. And don't wipe spilled bleach on your blue T-shirt.

That was the easy stuff; you will still have to keep the house somewhat clean. Now as a man you still will have some leeway on that whole clean versus cluttered thing. Let's start with what should be the hardest thing, the bathroom. First in my house it is my two boys and me. If this sounds like the living arrangements at your house I have a suggestion. You know that "U" shaped rug that sits in front of the toilet? Throw it away right now. Even if you are raising one boy, throw it away. If you have a daughter that wants it for sentimental reasons, I'm sure it would make a lovely wall hanging in her bedroom.

Men in general, much less little boys, are notoriously, well let's say bad shots? This rug will get and hold anything that doesn't make it quite into the toilet. When I say hold, I mean hold any corresponding odors too. You can only wash a rug so many times. It will be much easier for you to clean the floor on a regular basis than wash a rug every other day.

Let's go back to our trusty car. You know how you have that special rag or sponge you use on the car? You probably have a shammy cloth; towels you use, or in my case a blue bleach stained T-shirt, you use to dry it. You use car wash, your favorite wax, wheel cleaner and tire treatment. I keep mine in a five-gallon bucket in the garage.

Back to the bathroom. Lately there has been a number of very man friendly cleaning items come to the market. Two of these I find indispensable. Odd I would use that word because that is one of their greatest virtues, is that they are disposable. They come in a small re-sealable package. You pull open the package and pull out one pre-treated towelette at a time, similar to a tissue. You can use these to wipe down just about every surface in the bathroom, from the sink to the toilet and floor. When you are through with it just flush it away. There are also a number of cleaning products out that can be used to clean the toilet itself. I like the one that comes with a plastic handle to which you clip a small cleaning pad. This pad is impregnated with a blue, very nicely scented, cleaner. Again you use this product to clean the toilet bowl, and when done, just flush it away.

Using these products you can clean the bathroom in no time at all. If you use the wipes to clean the soap and water stain off the sink, and the floor around the toilet you will be pleased with you results. Unfortunately most bathrooms have more than just toilets and sinks. You will have to eventually clean the tub or shower. I have found the best way to do that is do two things at the same time. Spray your tub or shower with any of the readily available cleaners. I pick the ones that smell nice.

If you keep up on these I have found you can normally use just the product and the water from the shower to keep up with the cleaning. You will however have to occasionally have to scrub with either a brush, some-type of non-abrasive bleach added cleaner. If you start to get some mold or mildew build up in your shower, or anywhere else in the house for that matter, you will need to buy some cleaners that contain bleach. In the area of tubs and showers, they have a shower curtain. They sometimes need to be cleaned too. Most have two parts, a waterproof plastic liner, and a decorative exterior panel. The waterproof liner sometimes gets a little mildew on it. You can wash it in the bathtub with a little soap and bleach. If you can stand the smell and will have enough time for the bathroom to air out before it is used again, you can get inside the tub or shower stall and spray the plastic liner with a mold removing spray. Be careful the fumes on them are rough

Or you can be like me and put it in the washer with a lot of bleach and a little soap. If you do that remember that during the spin cycle, the water will not be spun out of the plastic liner. Guess what happens when you pull it out of the washer? You would just be amazed how much water a plastic shower liner can hold. That is of course that is until you start carrying it through the house.

Again men remember the house-cleaning fairy is not stopping at your house. You know that hand towel hanging in your bathroom? If you are not familiar with the concept let me put it this way, you are of course setting a good example of washing you hands after using the bathroom right? Well you need that towel hanging out where you can get to and use it. That towel needs to be replaced and washed, on regular bases. This goes for the washcloth you may keep in there too. While we are on that topic, all the wash clothes and towels used for showering have to be replaced and washed too. Just because they have a chance to dry out in-between uses, that isn't good enough. Regardless of what you think you might have learned from your pre-marriage days, dry does not equal clean.

There is another thing in every bathroom that needs cleaning. I would rather clean ten toilets than one of these things, the mirror. I only have two suggestions for cleaning them. The first would be to get a picture of your self and your children. Put it up in place of the mirror. Now you can see what you look like, so you don't need a mirror.

As much as I would like to give that a try we all know that won't work, so here goes. Use plenty of paper towels and as little window cleaner as possible. I have found that using more than the bare minimum only leads to streaking and that of course means more work for you.

Here is one last little tip for helping to keep your bathroom clean. The next time you go to the store buy a box of denture cleaning tablets. The kind that you drop in a glass of water and let your dentures soak all night as the tablet bubbles away. Take a few of these tablets and drop them into the toilet bowl. Do not put them in the tank; it could damage the internal workings of your toilet. It will bubble up and help keep the water and the bowl clean. It is also kind of neat the next time you have guests over and your bathroom has a "triple mint freshness" smell.

So far we have covered two areas most men would have trouble with, the laundry, and the bathroom. I am going to offend some house-cleaning purists with the next thing I am going to say, but here goes. While it is important to keep your house and clothes clean, there is one room in your house that has to be kept clean, the kitchen. While it is nice to have a clean house, and a fresh smelling bathroom, a dirty kitchen can have disastrous effects on your household.

Again use the routine maintenance theory. Clean as you go, keep up with your kitchen. I have a dishwasher in my kitchen and I don't know the last time I used it. I wash the dishes as I go. Unless you are entertaining a large group of people you probably are not going to have enough dishes to get a full load. What will happen if you just throw them in as you dirty them is this. You will try to make dinner one night and all of your dishes and pans will be in the dishwasher. It is just as easy to wash as you go. Don't forget you will have to dry them and put them away too. It will surprise you how quickly a few meals worth of clean dishes will fill up you sink. I know it surprised me.

Since the writing of this book I have used the dishwasher more often. There are times when you have to feed the kids and then run out to something at school. As I said with the clothes washer I have been known to wash a load in the dishwasher when it is not completely full. If you do this try to make sure you take out the clean dishes before you start putting in new dirty ones, or you will be washing a full load next time. There is also some argument as to using dry versus liquid detergent in your dishwasher. Many people tell me that their dishwasher tends to leak water onto the floor when they use dry or tablets.

Nothing says unprepared man lives here like a sink full of dirty dishes. They are easier to wash while the food is fresh. Use plenty of hot water and not too much dishwashing detergent. I like looking at the pretty bubbles too, but it makes them harder to rinse off. You will only have to drink something out of a glass or cup that still has liquid detergent in it once to learn a very valuable lesson. If you have never had the pleasure, I will tell you this. Remember all the work you just put into cleaning you bathroom? Well get ready to do it all over again.

As I mentioned earlier don't use steel wool to clean your dishes or pots and pans. First it will clean the non-stick finish off your pots and pans. Second, unless you plan on throwing it away after every use and getting out a new one they will rust, opening up a whole new area in cleaning. I have found the two-sided sponges work just as well. These are the ones that have a sponge on one side and a stiffer scrubbing surface on the other side.

If because of what you are having for dinner you cannot wash them right away, at least put any pots or pans used in the sink, and fill them with hot water, and a little detergent. Now if you are not familiar with cooking there are a few foods that you will wind up making that if not given immediate attention will cause you an undue amount of problems. Oatmeal, now oatmeal is good for you. I don't know about the half of a stick of butter and the cup of brown sugar you add to it, but oatmeal is healthy. Now if a food is known for "sticking to your ribs," what do you think it will do to the side of the pot you just made it in? Another food along those lines is macaroni and cheese. Hot gooey melted cheese, mixed with the boiled over starch from the noodles, burned onto a pan, nothing says clean me now louder.

These two make sense, I mean stick to your ribs, melted cheese, and they just have to be hard to clean. Well I want to mention two that may surprise you, first is egg yolks. Now these have to be real eggs not an egg substitute. If you serve sunny side up eggs, or over easy and don't clean your plate, not the pan they were cooked in, but the plate on which they were served, and don't at least rinse it you are in for some fun. I would have to say it is right up there with trying to scrub tar off the side of your car using a blue cotton shirt with bleach stains on it. The people that make crazy glue could learn a few things from the lowly egg yolk.

The other one I have found that is a real pain is Jell-O. I know there is always room for Jell-O, but not on the side of the pot you just made it in. I tried running it under the hottest water that would come out of the tap. Then it dawned on me that if the boiling water that was just in the pot left it there, the hot tap water probably won't help much. I'm sure you will have fun experimenting in the kitchen trying to find new and better ways to stick food to your pots, pans, and dishes, I know I am.

Be careful if the utensil used is glass. Did you know if you run cold water over a hot glass dish it will shatter? Neither did I. While on that topic here is another valuable life lesson I learned the hard way. There is a brand of glass cookware that claims it can go from the refrigerator or freezer to the oven. That does not mean it can go from the refrigerator or freezer to the burner on your stove top. Do you have any idea how hard it was cleaning leftover lasagna and broken glass out from around a hot electric burner?

I digress, back to cleaning in the kitchen. I will get into this more in the chapter with cooking, but this is important enough to mention more than once. As you are preparing your meals you will be preparing meats and vegetables. If during this preparation you use a cutting board, cut the vegetables first then meats. Wash it in between uses, but always cut your meat products last. If you should not do a thorough enough job, raw vegetable matter in your meat product will do no harm. Raw meat or blood products in you vegetables can be very bad.

I bring this up to introduce another product. There is any number of manufactures of disposable wipes. Some have bleach, some don't, and some are listed as killing bacteria on contact. I have even just bought some that have that nice orange scent to them. Killing bacteria in a kitchen would be a good thing. I know it seems like I keep pushing disposable items, well I am. You don't need a germ-laden washcloth lying around the kitchen. Clean up, throw them away, and move on. Wipe the counter tops down frequently. I keep a container of these wipes setting on my counter top.

There is a little known area in your kitchen that is one of the best, or worst, depending on how you look at it, places to grow germs. This place is used almost every day. Because this place is used in the preparation of so many different foods, it could have a very high-risk potential. Give up yet on where it is? Your electric can opener. The little blade on it goes inside every can you open. After a while it gets really bad. I will admit I didn't know about it either, until I read it somewhere. I thought yea right how dirty can it be? Very dirty. When I took it apart, I was stunned to see a thick black; well I don't know what it was, growing on the back of the little blade. I took it apart and washed everything thoroughly. I cleaned it so well that when I put it back together and had two parts left over. Luckily Target had one on sale; I had convinced myself I needed a new one anyway.

Another area I had to learn to clean the hard way is the area around and behind the faucet, or as we call them in Maryland, a spigot. It may frighten you what kind of filth will accumulate back there if you let it. This area includes the area between where the sink stops and the back splash begins. Now I know why they call it a back splash.

A lot of people would tell you to keep your cleaning supplies out of sight. OK if that is so, why do most of us have a fancy paper towel holder in plain sight in our kitchens? If there are small children in the house or even pets you will want to, of course, keep your chemical cleaners safely out of reach. I am OK with someone seeing a container of these types of wipes sitting out, maybe that means I will actually use them. Cleaning supplies are like your appliances. No matter how handy they are, out of sight means out of mind.

Now let's move onto the rest of the house. I mentioned dusting earlier, so let's start there. The first step in cleaning is dusting. No strike that, the first step in cleaning any room is moving a trash can into the room you are cleaning. Now you can start dusting. Here come the disposables again. I have found the new disposable dusters are great. The starter pack comes with an extendible handle. Why do you need an extendible handle? Here is a secret that I think women don't what us male house cleaners to know. Think about the last woman that looked at the cleaning job you did. Did you notice they looked up and at the floor? Well guess what? You need to extend that handle and dust the wall where it meets the ceiling. Dust the wall? No dust settles there. Oh yea? Well I tell you what; if you have never done it, try it. See all those cobwebs? Yes you did, don't lie. If you have been real lax in your cleaning you may even want to dust down the corners of the room while you're at it. The other area she was looking at was where the baseboard molding meets the wall. Dust collects there too.

If you are using the disposable dusters, they still need a little help. A quick spray of a furniture polish can't hurt. Be careful where you do that though. Furniture polish plus hard wood or laminate flooring plus feet in socks add up to really tough walking. Anyway start your dusting at the top and work down. Oh while you are dusting you will notice dust all over the TV picture tube. Do not dust that with furniture polish laden dusting clothes. For that job break out the paper towels and the window cleaner.

Now as a man I know you get a kind of perverse pleasure at looking how much dirt you just dusted from you walls and furniture. Fight it though. Change the dusting clothes frequently. Speaking about changing frequently, the floor. No don't change the floor. If you have any type of hardwood, laminate, tile, or linoleum flooring, ignore the advertising propaganda on the box of floor cleaners. They will not get your floor clean in one simple step, period. Here is when the trash can in the room starts to come in handy. On any of these surfaces start by sweeping them with a broom, and then use either a dustpan or a vacuum to clean that up. This will remove big stuff like sand and dirt. Then move on to the dry pads to go over the floor; check these frequently, and change them when they get dirty. Then and only then you can move on to the wet pads to clean the floor, checking these also, if they get too dirty they will leave streaks. See I told you that trash can would come in handy.

Let me make a quick trash can suggestion here. Save the bags when you go to the grocery store. Use them to line the smaller trash cans in the rooms in your house. Take several and put them in the bottom of the can. This works for any trash can you use liners in. Then put one in the can and just line the store bought liners. When you want to empty the can, just pull out the liner, take one from the bottom of the can, reline the can and go. It is even easy enough that I tell the boys to take out the bag and tie a knot in it every Monday and Thursday. Then just take a bag from the bottom and replace it.

I suggest this method of cleaning these surfaces for a few reasons. First it works. I know it looks like a lot of steps, but it goes by pretty fast if you do one room at a time. Second, if you try to vacuum these surfaces, you may scratch them. Most vacuum's that you use in the rest of the house have what is generically called a beater bar or beater brush. This is usually a belt or motor driven round brush at the end on the vacuum nozzle. The idea is that by agitating the carpet fibers you will get them cleaner. This theory works well on carpet, but on many of these other surfaces you can and will leave scratches, you don't want that.

Did you like how I brought up the topic of the vacuum cleaner? OK a quick review. All vacuums work through the principle of suction. Air being sucked through the vacuum hose will carry dirt with it into some-type of storage unit for disposal at some later time. First I will bring up things not to vacuum, especially if your vacuum has a beater bar or brush. Do not try to vacuum the fringed edges of a fringed area rug. Never try to vacuum the floor under a pair of shoes that have laces, without picking them up first. This goes for the floor under ties, belts; well I think you get the point.

I have found that for vacuuming the stairs, the little hand held vacuum I use to clean the inside of the car is best. They have longer cords and they are easier to handle on the stairs.

Now some places you will want to vacuum remember to use the attachment without the beater bar to vacuum the baseboard around the floor, remember the dust? Even though you cannot see it most of the time, you really need to vacuum under your bed, every time you vacuum. Here is another area most of us do not think about vacuuming. In your house, on every level there will be a large vent near the ceiling. This is the cold air return vent portion of your heating and cooling system. You will want to vacuum this vent, boy what dust magnet it is. If your closets are carpeted, they will get very dusty too; make sure to get in them.

Another feature of your vacuum must be addressed. In creating the suction needed to suck up the dirt, there is of course an inlet and an outlet. Before the air is released back into your house it will pass through some-type of filtration. Here I will break my rule of disposables. I like the bag-less vacuums. First you will never run out of bags. You will never have a bag explode the dried pine needles from your Christmas tree all over your house. Plus, yes I will admit it I like looking through the clear plastic container and look at all the dirt I just cleaned up. This plastic dirt cup comes in handy when looking for that small part to your son's favorite toy. Isn't it funny how you look at it as what a good house cleaner you are to clean up all that dust and dirt? Not what a poorhouse cleaner you to have let the place get that dirty in the first place?

A word of caution on your vacuum, no matter what kind you choose, bagged or bag-less the filtration needs to be kept clean if the vacuum is to work properly. Never under any circumstances are you to clean the bag-less holding area or change the bag inside your house. When you go out side to do this cleaning or bag replacement, make sure you are not standing upwind of an open door or window. Closed screens do not qualify as a closed window in this circumstance.

Try to think of your cleaning duties like you do routine maintenance, you can do a little work more frequently, or you are in for a major whole house cleaning.

Whole house cleaning is a bad thing. I have torn apart the whole house trying to get that one good cleaning of one room. You find yourself moving everything you can from the target room to some place else, another room. Now if you have just finished cleaning that room you may have a problem restoring that room.

Another product I cannot say enough about is the new spray fragrances, you know the ones you can spray on the carpet, the bed linens, curtains, just about any cloth, or fabric. Some of these now even come with antibacterial properties. This does not take the place of cleaning just freshens things up. There are certain times of the year when you can't or shouldn't open the window. During these times, even a clean house starts to get a little stuffy smelling.

One of these times, which an inexperienced house cleaner may not know about, is early spring. I know you are just coming off a winter of dry heat and are just dying to open the windows and air out your house. I live in the state of Maryland. While you may differ with me on this point, Maryland in springtime is the pollen capitol of the country. I have seen every surface in my house covered in green dust in the name of "airing out" my house. This really hurts your house cleaning efforts.

Speaking of dusting, cleaning and airing out your house, let me say two words, ceiling fans. I know you would never believe that a fan blade that spins in the air would get dirty. Well you would be right, they don't get dirty, they get filthy. Remember to clean them or you may learn another important household lesson. Ceiling fans have speeds and direction controls. Speed speaks for itself. The direction is used to make them work better at circulating the air in summer and winter. If you don't clean them a layer of dirt, dust and who know what builds up on the leading edge. If you don't clean them at least before you change the direction your nice clean room will be rained upon by big "globs" of dirty gunk. I think you get the picture.

The last thing I want to mention in the area of clean versus clutter is making the beds. As I said I do not want this book to be viewed in any way as spouse bashing, in that vein I will pay homage to my ex-wife. In the morning I, for the most part got the boys ready for school. One of the things she did every morning was make the beds. I have been doing this single parent thing now for over a year and still have trouble getting the beds made. I know what you are thinking; the boys could make theirs right? Well remember we are teaching our male children to keep a house clean. It is hard to make them make their beds when I forget half the time.

I however have a suggestion to help even with that. Get big comforters, bedspreads, and duvets, whatever you want to call them for every bed. Pull the sheets up as best as you can, and throw that comforter over the whole thing. Straighten that out; fluff up the pillows, and presto, made beds. Remember we are men we don't really know how to do this kind of stuff. Anyway as you, and I, get better at this housekeeping thing I'll start doing it the right way.

Something you may want to try is scented candles. Now as with everything there are trade offs. If you choose to use scented candles you have to remember to put them out before you leave. You have to remember to clip the wick every time before you light them again. If you don't, they will smoke and dirty up your nice clean house. Unlike dust, this soot will not just dust away, you actually have to wash or scrub it off. If it gets too bad it will even stain your ceiling. The only way to fix that one is to re-paint it.

They have started making candle melters. They look like a small crock-pot. The entire candle jar fits into the melter. Plug it in and presto, nice smelling house. This is especially handy around the holidays. A nice cookie smell at Thanksgiving and a nice pine scent at Christmas time especially if you have an artificial tree.

Now I will throw in one more man hint. If you are getting last minute company near Christmas time try this. Remember the clutter versus clean? Well pick up everything and move it into one room you don't plan on using. Then make a big sign that says: *Santa's Workshop: Do Not Enter.*

I want to mention one more product you as a single parent will want to keep around the house. Going back to your car cleaning history, most of us have had to clean the carpet on our cars at one time or another. They make a can that sprays foam carpet cleaner onto the carpet. The can has a brush on it either on the lid or as part of the can. You spray the carpet and then brush it with the attached brush. Trust me, when one of your boys gets sick at 3:30 AM and doesn't quite make it to the bathroom before he throws up, three times, you will be glad you can spray and clean the carpet while he is finishing up in the bathroom.

If like me your child also missed the toilet and has diarrhea at the same time, you can clean the carpet and use your disinfecting scrubby wipes on the floor in the bathroom. The good side is that my bathroom floor and the toilet got scrubbed three times that night, and the carpet in front of my bathroom has never been cleaner.

CHAPTER FIVE: EVERYDAY CHILD CARE

House keeping only accounts for a small portion of what you are now being called upon to do. You have to raise your children. By virtue of my two divorces I am clearly not the best husband in the world. I am sure that I am also far from the world's best father, but you don't have to be. Be the best one you can be, that is all that can be asked or expected from any of us. It doesn't matter how you or I for that mater found ourselves raising our children on our own. The fact is that you and I are here so let us strive to be the best job we can.

As I said this book was written to share my views and experiences as a single father raising two boys. I'm sure there will be variations of this. Some of you may have more or less children. There may be those with a girl or two or some combination of that. Keep in mind my point of reference.

As I started on the journey of single parenthood I sought out help from everybody I could find, that would talk to be about it. Another interesting thing along gender lines surfaced. I talked with a few male friends that were raising their boys. I seemed to be doing many of the same things they were doing with theirs. The things I wasn't doing that they were, I thought were for the most part good ideas too. The women on the other hand had a completely different view. All we men were coddling our children. We were doing too much for them. They all said we should make the kids do more.

Again I think this goes back to gender roles. In our society, the child raising has fallen mainly to the mother. In many instances if the mother is not available, the job of child raising goes to some other female, an aunt or grandmother or even a sister. This leaves the father or male relative as a person of last resort. This seems to have the trickle down effect of raising a generation of men that don't have the knowledge to deal with children. When put into the position of having to raise children we, men, have a tendency to overcompensate.

We feel we now have to do the job of two parents. While this may be true, it does not mean we have to do twice as much parenting. We do not have to do twice as much as the children were used to when both parents were in the family unit. Just try to keep things as close to the same as possible. Women seem to have a better handle on this than men.

I think that the first and most important thing is spending time with your children. I'm not sure this is the same thing as spending more time with your children. I spoke with Seth's therapist and she said time and time again, that the quality of time spent is more important than the quantity of time. In the evening just before Seth goes to sleep we spend fifteen to thirty minutes just talking. Sometimes we don't really talk about anything, just talk. I believe this type of interaction is better than a longer period spent sharing your time with other things. Spend time on what they like.

This can either be easier or harder than is sounds. When I find myself having trouble with this I try to remember this. If you meet one of your adult friends, you will find the two of you start talking about common interests. It may be fishing and hunting, camping, work, or maybe you share a hobby. Try to think of your children as small people. If your children have a favorite cartoon or TV character, you may very well have to learn something about that show or character. You could always ask them. They will be more than eager to tell you all about them.

As I have said my older son suffers from Asperger's syndrome.

One of the symptoms of Asperger's is that he has not matured emotionally at the same rate as other children his age. At night he likes to tell stories. He tells me stories about the shows he likes to watch. At times he tells me about the show he just watched; other times he uses his imagination. He makes up wild stories based on the various characters in his favorite shows. He does a great job, changing his voice as he talks as the different characters. A relative in Florida refers to him as the next Stephen King because of his vivid imagination. When it is my turn to tell stories, he asks me to tell him stories about the cartoons I watched when I was his age.

I have noticed that many of the cartoons I watched as a child are now available on DVD. Many of them are even making comebacks, reworked for a newer generation of children.

I believe your children want to talk to, and with you. They want you to talk to, and with them, but you have to understand their point of reference. They are not adults; they might like hearing an action packed story about something you did when you were younger. But I wonder if they enjoy it because it is action packed, or if it is because it is something you did when you were younger. When you were younger you probably had similar points of reference as they do at the same age. I am not saying you should only talk to them about things on a child's mind. You just have to be willing to do so.

One of the hardest things you will do as a parent is try to understand why a child is doing or saying something. My older son one-day told me he didn't want to go to heaven. I tried my adult logic on him. I told him when he gets to heaven he will get to see his grandmother and my grandparents, even his dog, Daisy. I told him about never getting sick and being able to live forever.

He again said he didn't want to go to heaven. My adult mind just couldn't understand why he would say such a thing. I even spoke with the pastor of our church about it. I thought coming from a preacher after all would have a stronger effect right? After a while I started to understand the logic of a child. Every one he knew of that was in heaven was dead. His grandmother died about five months after he was born. My grandparents were dead. His dog was dead. So in his mind I don't think he cared how wonderful heaven was. The only way to get there was to die, and he didn't want to die, the mind of a child. How can you argue with logic like that?

It is important to talk to your children about what you think are important values. I am a non-smoker. I think smoking is bad for you, and now so do my children. Just as it is important to talk with your children about things you feel are important, you must find out what is important to them and talk with them about that. Every child is different, even your own. What is important to one may not be important to the other.

Since your children now have only one parent doing full-time parenting, you will need to bring up another topic with them. They might have to answer the door or phone for you sometime. We used the Safe Side DVD, it was very good. It covers many topics you might not have thought to address.

I have been serious for a while; let's get back to something fun. I used to say when I was a police officer I was a trained observer. I don't know if that was true or not, but it sounded good to me. Because of shift work, being off for a back operation and since retiring I would find myself at the local mall. Have you ever noticed how many women you see at the mall with children? I assumed that was because the husband was working and couldn't make it, or some variation of that.

I think there may be another reason. First, just because you have your children that doesn't relieve you of your everyday duties. You still have to go shopping, run errands, everything you did before you became a single parent. Only now you are the only one doing them.

There is something else I have noticed. I think it is easier to entertain your children if you take them somewhere. Every mall has either a play area, or some child friendly stores you can go to. If you stay at home all the time, you wind up entertaining them. If you go out they wind up entertaining themselves. I guess it has something to do with all that external stimuli.

Remember when I mentioned that supper could be the most important meal of the day? Well there is another reason for that. Have you ever been in a restaurant and seen an unruly child? Well, don't blame the child. Children are just little adults; they will behave just like they are taught to. If you sit down with them over dinner and carry on an intelligent conversation at home, that is how they will behave if you go out to eat.

We try to go to church every week. We also try to go out to lunch every Sunday after church. The boys are dressed nicely, they behave well, and they are for the most part a pleasure to be with. Now here is a good place to put another friendly single parent warning. As I said we try to go out to lunch after church. One of our favorite places is TGI Friday's. It is kid friendly, and their kids menu is affordable and has some healthy choices. When we first started I had to remind them to behave themselves. They quickly learned this and behaved like little gentlemen. One day we went to a different restaurant. Seth started acting up a little bit. I called him on it and said, we talked about this, and you know how you're supposed to act when we are at a restaurant. Seth corrected me, no daddy, you said we had to be good at TGI Friday's. OK I stand corrected, be good at all restaurants.

This is part of our weekly routine. I think that establishing some sort of routine helps. Certain days are set aside for certain things. Sunday is Church and lunch afterward. Friday night we pick out a movie, pop some popcorn in the microwave oven and all watch the movie together. Monday's are busy with homework. We try to get a head start on it for the week.

I'm not saying that every day has to be written in stone. That isn't good either. If you are too structured, having one off day will throw off the rest of the week. However it gives them something to look forward to. They keep track of who picked the movie for last week and make sure they each get their turn. Another good thing about this is when you wind up having to discipline one of them; they have a concrete thing in their mind that they are going to lose while they are being punished.

Another thing you have to find out and fast are how to best spend your money, getting the most bang for the buck. This was driven home one day, when I had my two boys and a friend of theirs. We went to supper at a local fast food restaurant. As the boys were sitting there wearing their little paper crowns, I added up how much this meal was costing. The next week after church the same group of us went to a local buffet place. I had steak and pork chops. They boys ate a variety of pizzas, fried chicken, mashed potatoes, and green beans; well I'm sure you get the idea. We even had ice cream sundaes for dessert. The bill was only one dollar more than we had paid for the fast food meal.

While on the topic of eating out I found out something else that was split by gender lines. During our big summer vacation I planned as many meals at the trailer as possible; we would always eat breakfast at the trailer. If possible I would pack us a lunch. For supper we shopped the various, kids eat free, buy one-get one free offers.

During one of these nights out I learned another important lesson. Kids eat free doesn't really mean kids eat free. It means kids eat with a paying adult. Read that as kids eat free with each paying adult. So I still have to pay for one of them. I did find one restaurant where I was allowed to work out a deal. If I ordered a large cheese pizza, that was considered a meal that two adults would order. That way I got both the boys for free. We had half the pizza put in a box for take home, and all three of us shared the two kid's meals and half the pizza.

On the topic of budget eating make sure you always wear a watch. Most places, especially buffet type restaurants, have lunch prices and dinner prices. If you can get your family to eat an early supper, say before five o'clock, you normally get your supper for lunch prices. In my case it saves about ten to twelve dollars that your children will be only too happy to help you spend somewhere else.

One day while on vacation, I promised the boys we would go to The Greene Turtle. The Greene Turtle is a sports bar type restaurant at one end and regular seated dining at the other. We were seated ordered our drinks and the boy's food. Then like clockwork, we have to go to the bathroom. Of course the bathroom is located at the far end of the establishment. We went and I made sure everybody washed their hands and they left. I stayed behind to finish drying my hands and sent them back to the table. When I got back I noticed a damp white washcloth on the table. I tasted my raspberry-iced tea, and found it was no longer raspberry.

The boys pointed out the washcloth and said the man left it when he brought your drink back. What man I asked? He was like that one over there. When we went to the bathroom the bus boy had come to the table, cleared all of our drinks, wiped down the table and started gathering the place mats the boy's had just colored. Realizing his mistake he brought new drinks, but got mine wrong. By this time the waitress came over and apologized. I didn't really give it any more thought.

A few days later we went to another restaurant, The Olive Tree. This was more of a dining room only establishment. The waitress brought our bread and salad. Seth started in on the bread while Spencer and I had some salad. The waitress came back and we ordered our food. Trying to avoid a repeat of the Greene Turtle episode, I waited until we ordered. I figured they would see the half-eaten salad that is brought before every meal and realize someone was sitting there.

This time when we got back to the table, not only had the table been bussed and cleaned, but they already had new silverware on the table. The waitress made it back and fell over herself apologizing. I don't know if she was sorry or maybe saw her tip being cleaned off as fast as our table was.

Again I went to other single parents about this episode. Another gender difference on dad raising boys was uncovered. It seems like boys feel a genetically powered drive to go to every public restroom they possibly can. Girls on the other hand seem to have a pathological fear of them. As I was talking to other single parents I got advice like make them go before you leave, I did. I was told to let them go by themselves, one at a time. I can agree with that one with some provisions, if I can see the bathroom, if we have been to that restaurant before or I am in-between the bathroom door and the door to the restaurant. Keep in mind that I was still fairly new to this single parent stuff, we were pretty far away from home and didn't like letting them out of my sight.

I didn't really think any more about these incidents until I spoke with my daughter about it. She, like many college students waited tables for extra money. When she heard the story she said that happens all the time, to men. She said even during lunch two or three men would come in and order their drinks. When they see a table that had a group of men now empty they assume they have left and bus the table. If at the same time a table that was a group of women was empty they assume they are in the bathroom because we all know women travel to the bathroom in packs, or at the salad bar and don't bus the table till they either see the paid bill on the table or get word from the table's waitress. Again little gender differences in our society. I believe the way to prevent this is to make sure you tell your server if you are going to be leaving the table for bathroom breaks, or whatever

Staying busy with your children doesn't have to cost a lot of money. Baltimore City is home to the National Aquarium. During late summer and early winter you can go to the aquarium for only five dollars on Fridays after five, and it stays open until ten o'clock. The Maryland Science Center also offers lower priced admission plan Fridays after five. Washington DC isn't too far from where we live. There is no admission price to go to the Washington zoo. All you pay for is parking. While in Washington DC admission to any of the Smithsonian Institutions is free.

Remember I mentioned movie night? For the cost of admission to one movie for the three of us, not even counting concessions, we could rent movies all month long. I'm sure where you live there is something fun you can do with your children that cost little or nothing. There are county or city, public, parks everywhere. It doesn't seem to matter what you do with them, as long as you are doing something with them. They will find something they like to do.

One Saturday I packed a picnic basket and drinks. I took my two boys and again one of their friends for a day trip. About an hour away from our house is a hydroelectric power plant. The boys had been asking me if water could make electricity. They had seen it on one of their cartoons. So I thought this would be a nice ride, it would be informational and fun. I drove to the power plant, we drove across the top of the dam, and I showed them how high the water level was on one side of the dam as compared to the other. We parked below the dam and walked up almost to the base of it. There were people fishing where we were. You could hear the turbines turning in the powerhouse. I was trying to explain this to them, but they wanted to know what kind of fish people were catching. There were two carp that someone had caught tied up at the shore, the fish fascinated them. We finally left; I must admit I was a little disappointed. I thought they would like seeing the power plant, just like the one in their cartoon. In the same general area, upstream from the hydroelectric power plant was an even more amazing thing, a nuclear power plant, so we drove there. When we got there we ate our picnic lunch and I tried to tell them about the power plant and how it made electricity.

This plant and the hydroelectric power plant are both on the Susquehanna River. This is a major supplier of fresh water to Maryland and the Chesapeake Bay. The place where we had had lunch had a public boat launching ramp. At this launching ramp an "L" shaped floating pier had been constructed. Now so far for the day we had seen one of the largest privately owned hydroelectric power plants on the East Coast. We had also seen a nuclear power plant. What did my boys remember, talk about and what to do again? They wanted to go back and play on the floating pier.

What, you may ask is the moral of this little story? Well I planned a trip that I thought they would like. They liked it, but not for what I thought they would like, it didn't matter, they enjoyed themselves. Isn't that what the trip was supposed to be about anyway? The kids having a good time.

I have noticed something else. Now I don't know if this is unique to boys, single fathers or if it is the case in many situations like mine. I am surprised how fast two kids turn into three to four. Maybe they are looking for companionship. I don't know. I try to encourage them to have their friends. I think more therapy goes on with their peers than in any session. One of the boys mine play with Ben is also a child of divorce. I have over heard conversations covering stepmothers, stepfathers, and new marriages just about everything. We have to help our children, but they are smarter and more resilient that we give them credit for.

When I first found myself in this position, I tried to do everything for the boys. I washed, dried, folded, and put away all the laundry. I cleaned their rooms as I cleaned the rest of the house. Looking back maybe I was making work for myself. Was I trying to do more around the house to prove to myself that I was a good parent? As if to say, see I do everything around here? It didn't take too long to realize the boys were going to have to help too. I still wash, dry and fold but the putting away belongs to them. I have even started them on the moving clothes from the washer to the dryer.

I bought a large linen lined wicker basked for each boy's room. When they get undressed their dirty clothes go into the basket. If I see dirty clothes on the floor, I point it out to them but I do not pick it up for them. I have started letting them watch me do the wash. Before Spencer can really help, either he will have to grow a bit taller, or I need to get him a stool. Seth is tall enough. I will not expect them to do all the laundry, as long as I can do it I will. I may never trust them fully to do the white clothes. I can only imagine a spilled gallon of bleach. I'm sure whatever clothes it doesn't get on, will be used in an attempt to clean up the spill. I guess the good side to that would be that I wouldn't have to sort the clothes by color any more.

Here is a touchy topic even in households with both parents: discipline. I'll say it up front to get it out of the way. Yes, when I consider disciplining one of my boys, it does cross my mind that they will think their mother would have treated them better or at least handled it differently, so they should go live with her. So far I have not let that cloud my final decision. If they need disciplined, punished, I am their parent and it is my job to do it. If you do it out of love and fairness, not out of anger and a loss of control you will be fine.

Every child needs discipline. Discipline is not the same as punishment. Discipline means having structure, in your home or in society. In every relationship one parent always seems to draw the short straw and become the disciplinarian for the family. The other one gets to be the one the children run to for comfort. Now you get to be both. I have tried to be honest and have told them how bad it makes me feel when they are bad. I got my share of discipline when I was younger. I wonder if the idea of "this hurts me more than it hurts you" sounds as lame to my boys when I say it to them, as it did when my father said it to me?

I have given you some insight into my older son; Seth, now let me introduce you to my younger one Spencer. When I was a little boy, one year I received a toy, plastic tool set. One of the tools in it was a little plastic saw. I bet the manufacturers of that little plastic saw would never have believed you could cut the arm off of a couch with it. In my house I have a fireplace. In front of the fireplace I have a few pieces of marble that serve as a hearth. I have a piece of stained trim in-between the marble and the hardwood laminate flooring in the rest of the room. One day my little boy was being quiet, too quiet. I started looking for him. Well I found him in the family room. You see someone had given him a little toy plastic tool set as a gift. I bet the manufactures of that saw would have never believed you could cut through the trim on the floor with it. I was not pleased but what could I do? I explained to him that was wrong, we don't use the saw inside anymore.

I have since found that if I am using any of my tools and he is around I have to set up some comparable job for him to do. Once I started a bunch of screws in a piece of scrap wood. He sat there all day long with my cordless drill running the screws in and out of the wood. I refer to him as God's little reminder of everything bad I did as a kid.

Now to show you that behavior like mine and Spencer's runs in the family it is time for a little story. My grandfather was raised in rural Germany. One day he and his uncle went into the woods to catch birds and eels to sell. As they were walking through the woods my grandfather saw a "little baby pig." Remember we are in rural Germany many years ago. The "little baby pig" was actually a baby wild boar. My grandfather was advised to leave the little piggy alone. Well, in a little while a large sow wild boar came charging out of the woods straight toward my Grandfather and his uncle. The boar chased them up a tree. As they were hanging from tree branches, my grandfather's uncle asked, "Willie, wear is the piggy?" My grandfather opened up his coat and, smiling, said, "Right here." I am told the boar kept them in the tree quite a while even after they returned he baby.

If you have younger children I found another little trick that helps.

My boys have a wide variety of movies. I would check to see how much time I had before the next event, going to bed for example. If it was Friday and movie night it didn't matter as much. If it were a school night I would start at their bedtime and count back to the current time. Then I would pick a movie that would be over around their bedtime.

This is also a good thing to keep in mind for long trips. You can put a longer movie on and keep them occupied for most of the trip. I tried the driving games with some success. But again if you are the only adult in the car, maybe you should be paying attention to your driving. Of course you could always go low tech. I have been told there are things made out of paper that you read, I think they are called books. You could even give them brochures of wherever it is you are going. Give them the chance to pick out some things they think they would like to do once they get there. You could always try what our parents did, leave at o'dark thirty and let them sleep through most of the trip.

CHAPTER SIX: LOOK OUT, THERE'S A MAN IN THE KITCHEN

We discussed earlier some methods you can use to help keep your kitchen clean. Now let's talk about the real fun topic, how to get it dirty. As earlier we will assume that the average man will not be real familiar around the kitchen. Again there are some things you must first become familiar with before you can do any creative cooking.

We have already covered briefly the stove, oven, and some other kitchen appliances. There are some other fundamentals I think we should cover, first are measuring devices. Should you discover you are missing these you might want to think about replacing them.

The professional chefs on TV can estimate things fine, but odds are the average single father is not a professionally trained chef. Make sure you have a set of measuring cups. They come in one quarter, one-third, one-half, two thirds, and one-cup sizes. The reason I mention this is that I don't want you to try a recipe that asks for a cup of an ingredient and you confuse a measured cup for that thing you drink coffee out of. That is most likely a mug. A cup is only eight liquid ounces, that's only about two thirds of a can of soda. Another thing that I should mention here is there is a difference between eight ounces and eight ounces. Really you might say? Yes, there is a difference in liquid and dry weight ounces. That may be a while off, but is useful to know.

Another thing to consider is measuring spoons. You might get away using a real teaspoon or tablespoon as your measuring spoons. That is of course until you are asked to add one eighth of a teaspoon of something, that could get very messy real fast.

We will also assume that not only is the average man not familiar or comfortable in the kitchen, but is short on time, between work and your responsibilities to your children. There are some other labor savers you might want to get to know. These not only assist in the preparing on your meal, but in the clean up.

I like using the clear plastic bags in the oven. Not just clear plastic bags that would be messy. These are clear bags made to be used in the oven. Chickens and turkeys are easy and taste great when prepared in them. Roasts are almost too easy. Put in your roast, a few potatoes, onions, carrots, celery, and a bag of dry onion soup mix and throw it in the oven, in a pan of course. Not only is that a one pot meal but if you are careful cutting the bag open and getting out the roast and veggies, clean up will consist of a trip to the trash can. These bags are now even available for use in crock-pots or slow cookers.

Make aluminum foil your friend. I line baking sheets, cookie sheets and even the bottom of my oven. Depending on what kind of stove top you have you can line the burners with aluminum foil. Use it in the toaster oven too. Even with a self-cleaning oven, you don't want the extra large double cheese pizza bubbling all over the bottom of your oven. Speaking of self-cleaning ovens, if you never used one brace yourself. The phrase "self cleaning" is like the aforementioned non-stick and waterproof. The oven doesn't really clean its self, it cleans by heating up the oven to as hot as it can for a few hours and basically burning everything in the oven to dust. You then open the oven and wipe out a layer of dust left behind.

Once I tried making a big cookie, not a big batch of cookies, a big cookie. Needless to say my cookie turned into an episode of I love Lucy. It expanded and expanded right over the sides of the pan I was using. There was as much cookie dough on the bottom of my oven as there was in the pan. Did I even try to clean any of it out? Of course not, I'm a man, self-cleaning oven, do your stuff.

I had to open every window in my house, turn on the vent over the stove, and the whole house fan. After about an hour or so I then got to go around the house and put the batteries back into all of the smoke detectors in the house. I guess the moral of this story is avoiding a mess in the first place is easier than cleaning it up afterward.

Along with aluminum foil there is a product called parchment paper. You can find it in the same isle in the grocery store as the aluminum foil. It will either come in a roll or in sheets. This product is also useful for lining pans before baking. Just make sure you trim the ends so they don't hang over the edge of the pan, paper in an oven and all. Anything like biscuits, rolls and the like, come out great with parchment paper.

While on the general topic of the oven, you will want and need a good set of oven mitts. These too come in a few types. The traditional oven "mitt" looks just like the cold weather mitts you wear, only thicker. I like these because they give you thumb control. The other is more of a "pot holder." It doesn't really hold pots. It looks like a square of quilted material. They are nice for leaving on the lid of a covered pot, that you will of course check all the time. It is surprising how hot pans are when the come out of an oven. Maybe that is what they mean when they say it is "hot as an oven in there."

These are needed not just for the oven, but for removing the lid from a pot on the stove with some kind of boiling liquid in it. Water boils at 212 degrees, so how hot do you think that steam-covered lid is? I have tried using a folded towel, but ever since it came unfolded and fell back onto the burner and caught fire, I stopped doing that. Another quick tip is when you are removing the lid from the boiling pot, tilt it toward the front, that is raising the back of the lid first. That way you allow the steam to escape away from you instead of all over your arm and any liquid that falls off the lid falls back into the pot.

In the same line of hot pots, pans or cookware you will need something to put under them before you set them on your counter or tabletop. Your potholders will work great for that.

Another thing to beware of in the kitchen with your oven mitts is water. I like to kind of clean up the kitchen as I go. Of course with cleaning dishes comes water soap that kind of stuff. One time I grabbed my oven mitts and put them on. I noticed they were wet, but like a man thought, water feels cool this should work even better. Remember the water boils at 212 degrees we just talked about? Guess what happened when the 400-degree hot baking dish hit the water in the oven mitts. I thought I steamed off a layer of skin, again, not a good idea.

As I said earlier it is important to spend time with your kids, and supper is a great opportunity. Now in our society a family meal is unique. Again back to the one true barometer of society's values, TV commercials. In one, a husband and wife stand in the dining room with a bucket of chicken, and call their children, "Kids, supper time." The kids come running and screaming down the stairs, past the parents, through the kitchen, and into the van in the driveway. Funny but true, my favorite kind. So if you don't want your house to wind up like a TV commercial, you will have to venture into the kitchen.

Before you start cooking there are certain staples you will want to keep around your house. There are a few that keep well, can be used to make many different meals, and most of these are fairly easy to make.

Keep several types of pastas. You never know you might have a son like Spencer. One day we were choosing what kind of pasta to make for that evening. First Spencer picked some thin spaghetti noodles. Then he saw we had a box of twisted noodles. He said he wanted that one, because it is easier to get more of them on the fork at one time. I also keep several jars of pre-made spaghetti sauce in the pantry.

Seth is not a big spaghetti eater, so sometimes I have to make concessions. For example I keep a large bag of frozen ravioli in the freezer. I boil one pot of water with whatever pasta Spencer and I will be eating; in another pot I boil the water for Seth's ravioli. Then I heat up the spaghetti sauce in another pan. When they are done I plate the pasta and Seth's ravioli. Then I put the spaghetti sauce on mine, Spencer's and Seth's. The remaining sauce makes a nice dipping sauce for mozzarella cheese sticks.

Some nights I have even gone so far as to make some sort of pasta by itself. We call it pasta night. Then Seth just puts butter or cheese on his. Spencer either wants "red" sauce or cheese or butter. I like mine with a little olive oil, garlic and some Italian seasonings. You can use the bottles of squeeze cheese to make a plate of macaroni and cheese right on the plate. Then you get whatever you want on yours and everybody gets what he or she wants and you still only dirty one or two pots.

If you really feel like going all out Italian you can buy an un-sliced loaf of bread at the store. Slice it into thick slices once you get it home. Take some butter and whip it with a little garlic. You can get it in small jars already prepared for you. If even that is too much for your first outing, try butter and sprinkle a little garlic powder over them. Take your garlic butter and spread it on the slices of bread, then pop them into the toaster oven for a little bit. When they come out you can sprinkle them with a little dried shredded Parmesan cheese, presto home made Italian bread.

There are other staples that you have to have. Cans of corn, green beans, or any other vegetables you and your kids like, boxes or bags of rice, macaroni and cheese, boxed potatoes and the aforementioned pastas in a bag. There are purists that will tell you they all have too much salt or something else equally bad for you. Sometimes however money and time require you to get what you can.

There are some things you want to keep in your freezer too. I keep bags of chicken breasts, both boneless, skinless and breaded chicken tenders, fish sticks are always good too. In the fish stick arena, if your kids aren't crazy about them, you can always put a slice of cheese on them. One slice nicely covers four fish sticks. There are also battered and breaded fish filets your kids should enjoy. You can also get bags of French fries, or potato puffs that you can bake in the oven.

There are good pizzas for one that you can get. They are just enough for one kid and although they only come in cheese, it is easy enough to let them pick out their own toppings. Pizza bagels and pizza rolls round out your freezer very nicely on pizza night.

Most stores also now sell, in the frozen foods section, large soft pretzels. They can be a good base for a meal or snack. They are pretty good by them selves, but they readily accept cheese, crab meat, pizza sauce, just about anything you could put on a piece of bread or pasta could be used.

You may want to keep some taco kits around and some tortilla shells. On Mexican night you can make easy tacos and then sprinkle shredded cheese on a tortilla shell. You then fold them in half and back to your trusty toaster oven, and presto, quesadillas.

Another easy meal is an oldie but a goody. Again this may offend the purists, but if they don't like it maybe they would like to come over and cook for us some time. Take big baking potatoes wash them off, stick them several places with a fork, and wrap them in clear plastic wrap. Put them in the microwave oven and press the potato button. They are done when you can stick a fork into them and it goes in very easily. Then take them out of the plastic wrap and again look for the toaster oven. Put them in until the skin starts to "toast" up. The rest is up to you and your kids, cheese, sour cream, butter, cheese and broccoli, or go for the gusto, cheese, broccoli, and bacon. They make a great all in one meal, taste good, and easy clean up what more could you ask for.

Living in Maryland, you would assume seafood would feature prominently in our meal preparation. I was however raised on a small farm where we grew our own beef. That plus being first generation German means meat and potatoes are more likely to be on my plate than seafood.

I have found another thing the boys like and is an easy fix, crab cakes. By saying what I am about to I will probably get my "live near the Chesapeake Bay" card revoked but, I buy pre-made and prepackaged crab cakes. They are full of filler and very lightly seasoned. The boys however like and eat them, and they, the crab cakes, are an easy fix inside your trusty toaster oven. This meal works well with oven baked French fries sprinkled with seafood seasonings.

Spencer will eat cold crab salad made from imitation crab meat, Seth will not. I try to keep either a container of crab salad, tuna fish, or chicken salad made and in the refrigerator for quick meals. You can get cans of chicken or turkey in the store near where you find the tuna fish.

Another thing that will help with meals is if you pay attention to what your children are watching on TV. The main character in a popular cartoon the boys like, works as a fry cook making sandwiches, more specifically crabby patties. A local restaurant serves them as part of their menu. One of the boys got one and I looked at it to see how it was prepared. It was nothing more than a hamburger, lettuce, tomato, and cheese. On top of the cheese they sprinkle a seafood seasoning called Old Bay, I'm sure any brand would do though.

One night the cartoon network was having Cheese Night. I know Cheese Night? What did you expect from the Cartoon Network? Anyway I got a small cheese assortment and as they had different cheeses on the show, we would follow along at home.

If like me you are raising boys try a Sloppy Joe night. They are easy to make and of course boys like anything with the name "sloppy" in it. Plus you get another one-pan meal. This meal goes well with oven baked fries.

There are other ways to stretch your budget and get good meals at the same time. On a recent trip to the grocery store I wanted to get some ham steaks. They were $3.59 a pound. Now right next to them, in the same case was a whole ham butt for $1.49 a pound. Not only was it the same type of ham it was actually the same brand, just not cut into slices. I buzzed the butcher and had him cut it into ham steaks, and left a butt for making ham, green beans, and potatoes. This works well for getting large frozen turkeys cut in half too. Most stores run ads for frozen turkeys sometimes as low as $0.59 a pound. However they want you to buy a very large turkey. Much bigger than you would cook on any day other than Thanksgiving. Sometimes they would even be too big for that, but half would be just fine. I'll cover more on budgeting later.

In an effort to expose your children to more, different kinds of foods, you might have to get creative. One night I tried a blend of vegetables called California Blend. It is a mixture of carrots, broccoli, and cauliflower. Seth did great on the broccoli, but was a little slow on the rest. I had seasoned them a little too much so I was glad he ate any at all. I told him he had eaten enough, but to try one piece of cauliflower. He said OK I'll eat one piece of the "cottonflower." Well who cares what he calls it if he eats it.

I have also found it easier if you put the food on the plates instead of putting it in bowls and letting everyone serve them selves. This makes less clutter on the table and gives you more control over portions. You can also then make direct comparisons on showing them how little of, insert whatever your children are not fond of here, compared to everything else on the plate.

There is a school of thought that suggests a cooking day, lets say Saturday or Sunday. You cook a big pot of spaghetti, let it cool, and put it in bags or containers for the week. Baked chicken or turkey will last you a week very nicely too. You could make tuna, chicken, crab salad, or whatever your family likes and again put it away for later in the week. I also keep some frozen kids meals in the freezer too, for those nights or days when time just flat out gets away from you.

Along the line of teaching your kids, I have started having the boys make their own meals. This is of course with my supervision. I bought a bag of prepared dried chicken noodle soup. There are directions printed on the back. I had Spencer put the right amount of water into a pot I got for him. Then he cut open the bag and added the ingredients and whisked them together. I turned on the stove and brought it to a boil. Then we added some rice and some extra noodles. We added a few extra cups of water. Spencer set the timer and 20 minutes later his soup was done. Spencer loved telling everyone what good soup he made. I had to buy Spencer a little stool so he could reach the stove but it was more than worth it.

Normally this calls for the addition of chicken or turkey, but we just made it with the noodles and rice. If you are making it, feel free to add whatever you want, more vegetables, chicken, turkey, rice, noodles, whatever you like. This works well in a crock-pot too. When making soup I prefer chicken thighs. They are inexpensive, give the soup a good flavor and the one bone pulls out after cooking over night.

Seth has started making his own grilled cheese sandwiches. I get out the electric griddle and then tell him what to get out. He puts the sandwiches together squirts butter on them and puts them on the griddle. When it is time he flips them. I might be wrong but they seem to enjoy the food a little more when they fix it themselves.

Pancakes are a great breakfast. With a little practice you might be surprised the different shapes you can make with the batter. Pancakes are very easy to customize too. Chocolate chips, blueberries, diced apples, strawberries all go great with them. We make chocolate, chocolate chip pancakes from a mix we get from Trader Joe's, a local grocery store. The boys like them so much, they eat them with nothing on them.

Don't try to get that fancy with waffles. For the most part pancake mix and waffle mix are interchangeable. The main difference is that waffle mix usually adds a small amount of oil to the mix. I have tried making chocolate, chocolate chip waffles as well as just chocolate waffles. Let me say that they didn't quite turn out as planned. They stuck to both the top and bottom of the waffle iron. They even melted to the waffle iron, making clean up a real mess.

There will be times you will be forced into resorting to a frozen meal. When you buy these standbys, remember frozen food is not always fast food. I bought a family size box of frozen lasagna. Luckily I looked at the cooking directions when I bought it. It had to cook for almost one and a half hours. Certainly not what you want to pull out of the freezer for a last minute meal. Even at that it was hardly set it and forget it. Cut slits in the plastic top and bake for one hour, then remove the plastic and continue baking for another twenty minutes. Of course it was much cleaner than making the mess with several bowls I would have had to use to make lasagna from scratch.

CHAPTER SEVEN: WALT DISNEY WORLD

When my daughter Amy went from 5th to 6th grade my parents and I took her to Walt Disney World for her graduation from Elementary School to Middle School. To keep things fair I did the same for Seth in the summer of 2006, as he graduated from 5th to 6th grade.

I looked into what would be the best, most affordable, time conscious, convenient trip. Of course money is always a consideration, but I have found that when you are the only adult you have to take into consideration the convenience factor. Since I knew the location of the trip I next had to decide how best to get there.

I looked into driving. Mapquest put the trip somewhere around 910 miles from our house. It estimated a nerve soothing 14 hour and 8 minute journey. That of course does not take into consideration stopping for gas, meals, bathroom, and sanity breaks. As I mentioned earlier I have had my back fused. This added to the formula. If I drive I not only need 4 to 6 extra meals, but a night in a hotel down and back and carrying luggage from the car, to the room and back for one night.

Now if I tried to drive straight through, would I miss a day in Orlando while my back tried to recover from the drive? At the time of this trip, gas in Maryland was a thrifty $3.10 a gallon. I have a Ford Excursion that on a good day with a strong tail wind, going down hill gets about 14 miles per gallon. If all I did was drive there and back I estimated about $400.00 in gasoline alone, plus the cost of two nights in a hotel, and the accompanying meals and it became about a $50.00 difference to fly. From Baltimore that would cut the trip from 14 hours to 2 hours, talk about a no-brainer.

Now I understand that this may sound like a commercial for Disney, but it isn't. Disney does however offer some very nice perks. Universal Studios in Orlando also offers some convenient options but for now I can only talk first hand about Disney World.

When you book through Disney they now offer something they call Disney Magic. No it is not Mickey waving a magic wand and making all your money disappear. See I told you this wasn't a Disney commercial. If you choose the Disney Magic package you only have to get you, your kids, and your luggage to the airport from which you are leaving. Disney sends you tags for your luggage. Two tags per person. You attach them to your luggage and get them to the airport. The next time you see them they will be in your room at Disney almost like, well magic.

You must also decide where you want to stay. They have rooms from the affordable, $79.00 a night, to the ludicrous, somewhere around the $2,000.00 a night range. I'll give you one guess which end of the range we choose. We stayed at the All-Star Sports Resort. The room was like a standard hotel room you are used to. We had two full sized beds, tub, sink, all the standard stuff. There are two pools and a kiddy pool. At the bathhouse there are facilities for washing your laundry.

While we are there, a girl's softball league was staying at the resort. There always seemed to be someone in there washing uniforms for the next day's games. I used that as my excuse for not doing the clothes before we came home. But it is a nice feature to have if you needed it.

Interestingly enough at the All-Star Resorts, there are three of them, All Star Sports, All Star Music and All Star Movies, if you want a small refrigerator in your room, you have to pay extra. It would have been nice to have a refrigerator in the room but they have another nice feature. You buy a refillable mug for around $13.00. The resorts have what they call drink stations, you can refill the mugs for the entire length of your stay for free. After about 20 minutes in the Florida sun, you will drink your $13.00 worth of drinks the first day.

Depending on the age of your kids, there may be another very nice feature that you will make use of. By staying in a Disney resort, you receive what Disney calls Extra Magic Hours. Every day a different park opens an hour early only to people staying in the Disney resorts. One day at the Disney Animal Kingdom, we did about three of the "big" rides even before the park opened to the general public. Now every day another park stays open up to three hours late. One of the nights we were there, the Magic Kingdom stayed open till 2:00A.M. All of the rides aren't open, but all the rides you will want to ride will be. Because of their age we didn't take advantage of those hours, but I can only imagine what the Magic Kingdom must look like at 1:00 A.M.

As a guest at a Disney resort, you are also initialed to use their transportation. That includes transportation from and back to the airport in motor coaches, as well as transportation to and between all the Disney theme Parks, most of this transportation is provided by busses, but you can also make use of the boats and the monorail.

To make the most of this, you will want to get an upgrade on the standard tickets. You will want to get the Park Hopper Option. The basic ticket gets you into any park, but only one park a day. By upgrading you can start the early "magic" hour in one park, go back to your room for an afternoon nap and then go back to a different park and take advantage of the extra hours at night. In effect hopping from one park to another, hence the name, Park Hopper Pass. Based of course on the age of your children, you may want to sleep in and then stay late at the parks. My boys were done in by about 9:00 every night. I wasn't far behind them.

This covers some of the basics, so I will get into some of the specifics of our trip. We arrived at the Resort around noon. Our room was not yet ready. We were still allowed to check in, and given the cards that would serve as room key as well as our tickets to the parks, but not the room number. We had packed a carry on bag with swimming suits and such in it. We changed in the large bathhouse and went swimming for a while. While we were swimming they "checked" the two pieces of carry on luggage we had. It was secured in a locked room and we were given a claim check for it. About 1:30 Spencer and I checked on the room. It was ready and we headed to the room. Our luggage from the plane as well as the checked luggage was in our room waiting.

I didn't want to use a day of our park hopper on what would be a partial day so we took a bus to Downtown Disney. If you have older kids, you know like 18 to 21 or you like to shop, Downtown Disney is the place for you. There are loads of stores and several upper end restaurants, a movie theater and a cirque de Sole`. As part of our package we were given a coupon for a free adult meal and drink at Planet Hollywood. We had supper there and looked around for a while.

Downtown Disney is home to Pleasure Island. Pleasure Island is home to several different types of bars and comedy clubs. Also in the Downtown Disney area you will find DisneyQuest Indoor Interactive Theme Park. Disney describes it as "five floors of interactive rides and games." We did not go in because it would have been just shy of one hundred dollars just for admittance. This is another area where you might want to look at an upgrade.

Again you know the ages and likes of your children. If this is something you think they would want to do, you have the option to upgrade your Park Hopper again to include with the "Water Park Fun & More" option, you can choose admission to DisneyQuest Indoor Interactive Theme Park, as an option. We did not have that option as I was just hoping to get through the theme parks. I did not think we would get to the water parks. Based on my observations, if you have younger children and you do not drink and are not on the U.S. Olympic shopping team I would recommend staying at the Resort and resting up for the next day. If your kids are set on starting and you get there early enough, you could go to the park that is offering late magic hours.

Taking advantage of the early hour the next morning we went to

Disney's Animal Kingdom. The scheduled time for the parks opening is 9:00 A.M. We were in line and in the park by 8:00. The employees, sorry they like to be called cast members, were very helpful with suggestions of which rides to get on before the park opens to the general public arrived. In the Animal Kingdom we were able to ride the parks three major attractions before the regular 9:00 opening time. We were some of the first to ride the first ride, DINOSAUR. We rode the new Expedition Everest-Legend of the Forbidden Mountain with very little wait and again almost no wait for the Kilimanjaro Safaris. Expedition Everest would be the first and last roller coaster type ride the boys would ride during this trip.

It was our second ride and it started already. Two boys, one dad, and each seat only holds two people. I struck up a conversation with the gentleman in line behind me. Luckily he was also by himself, so I rode with Spencer and he rode with Seth in the car behind us. Both boys admitted, however grudgingly that they did like it some, but not enough to get back on.

Somewhere between the DINOSAUR ride and the Everest ride we somehow lost the battery to our camera. Maybe take a spare, the battery cost us $18.00. We then got on the Kilimanjaro Safaris. This was a very nice ride; you will want to get on this ride early. Just like us when the rest of us animals, the animals in the tour get hot and tired in the Florida sun. We got some great close up pictures of hippopotamus, elephants, lions, all the animals you would expect to see on an African safari. For your best bet at seeing more animals, go early.

We did a walking tour, took a few pictures, and headed back to the room. We had a quick lunch and all took a short nap. After we woke up we headed out to another park. We continued this for a few days. However the heat and excitement of it all started to wear on everybody. We stayed with the going to the park that opened early, but stayed later and by the time we got back to the room we called it quits for the day.

For smaller children the early hour open is at least from our trip, the best bet. However there is another feature that bears mentioning.

Disney has a program called the FASTPASS. The FASTPASS is available on most of what would be considered the big-ticket rides. The ones everybody wants to do. On most of these rides you will see posted a wait time. That time is called the stand by wait time. One of the rides in EPCOT was once listed as 120 minutes of in line wait. To use the FASTPASS you take your room key/ticket and go to a FASTPASS dispenser. You put in your room key/ticket and you receive a small coupon or FASTPASS.

The FASTPASS will give you a time range in which to return to the ride. It is about an hour window for you to return and use the pass. Also listed on the FASTPASS is the time you can get another FASTPASS for another ride or attraction. Check the time on the FASTPASS and the time the next available lot of FASTPASSES will become available. On one occasion we tried to get a FASTPASS for the ride SOARIN'. It was about 2 P.M. I looked and it said that the next lot of FASTPASSES that were available was for 7:45 P.M. We didn't ride SOARIN' that day.

When you get a FASTPASS and it is in the correct time window, you return to the ride or attraction and go into the FASTPASS line. For the most part there really is little or no wait. If you plan to visit Disney World, I also suggest you get the brochures of each park and the schedule of times for any show you might want to see. One day while in the MGM studios we attempted to get a FASTPASS to see Lights, Motors, Action. By noon all the FASTPASSES for the day had already been issued. We waited until we came back another day for that one. Again a quick tip, if you miss Lights, Motors, Action, the Power Rangers are available at the same time. At least that is how they were scheduled while we were there.

Again you will have to base which parks you spend most of your time in on the age and sex of your children, the length or your stay and your overall budget. Very young children will probably spend more time on The Magic Kingdom. As they get older you will find other shows and attractions that would better suit them. Disney offers a very comprehensive vacation planning DVD that I would also highly recommend.

Again based on the ages and maturity of your children there is another program you could try. I did not take advantage of it and had to call them back to check for this writing. There is a program were if two parents and two children wanted to go on a ride they are allowed to do a ride sharing type of arrangement. In the traditional setting one parent and one child waits in line and rides the ride. The other parent can then "share" and get right back in line with the child with out waiting in the line a second time.

I asked if this type of scenario would be possible. If a single parent and two children were to be at the park. One child could wait at the exit line and the parent and other child could ride the ride. When the ride was over the parent could "share" the ride with the other child. This program was of course set up for parents with a younger child that couldn't ride a ride and would have to be watched by the other parent. If your children are old and responsible enough and you would be comfortable leaving them at the exit by themselves, I was told that you could take advantage of this program. You would simply have to tell the cast member as you and the first child were getting on the ride. Then when you get off your first child waits while you and the second child ride.

Speaking of asking a cast member, we went to the Hawaiian Luau at Disney's Polynesian Resort. Seth was most pleased by the fact they sang songs from the Disney movie, Lilo and Stitch. Spencer, I should have only been so lucky. Spencer liked the part when the cast member came out and was twirling the flaming swords. At one point he put out one of the swords and touched the lighted one to his tongue. His tongue then was "on fire" and he transferred the fire to the other sword, setting it back on fire. The whole time I was having visions of Spencer trying this at his next birthday party. The luau was a little on the pricy side, but I think it was worth it and would do it again.

After the luau we walked along the sand to the Grand Floridian Resort Hotel to catch the monorail back to the Magic Kingdom and our ride back to our Resort. We were the first in line and I grabbed, well more like got the attention of, a cast member at the monorail station. I will let you in on another neat thing you can do. I asked him if anyone had asked to ride in the front of the monorail yet. When I say front I mean like in the front, in front of the driver. If you get the vacation planning DVD you will see what I mean. No one had asked yet so we got it. We got up front with the driver, he asked where we were going, and I hated telling him the very next stop. I asked him how far he was allowed to take us. He said he could take us one time around and drop us back off at the Grand Floridian Resort Hotel. I agreed and off we went.

After a quick stop at the Magic Kingdom we headed off to the Contemporary Resort. If you don't know what this one is, it is one of the original resorts at Disney World. The resort is built like a large A frame. The monorail goes right through the middle of the building. And we were right up front, the first ones in the building. We got a great view of the Polynesian Resort as we coasted by. We then were back at the Grand Floridian. The boys just loved the fact they were up there. Their dad kind of liked it too. Just remember to ask.

Another suggestion I would make is to schedule character meals, either breakfast or lunch. You have to schedule these with Disney when you plan your vacation. Except for the Luau, and a few specialty shows, you do not pay for them until you attend the meal. We scheduled ours for Breakfast with Donald Duck at Restaurantosaurus in Disney's Animal Kingdom. It was called Donald's Breakfastosaurus in the DinoLand U.S.A. section of the Animal Kingdom. We were seated quickly for a buffet breakfast. There are a number of reasons I recommend doing this. First, as I said the Animal Kingdom opens at 9:00 A.M. Our Breakfast was scheduled for 8:15 A.M. We were inside the park before it opened. This was not one of the days the park opened early. The other reason was that the entire Disney gang met us at our table, Donald Duck, Pluto, Goofy and Mickey Mouse I was able to get pictures with them and the boys seated at our table, Inside an air conditioned restaurant.

You know that you will eventually have to get the obligatory picture with the Disney characters, so you have two choices. You can schedule a character meal and take your pictures when the characters come to you. They will pose with your children and you can take your time. Or you can wait till one of these characters is brought out into one of the parks. You can then stand in line in the heat, waiting your turn; your choice.

Like I said earlier wear a watch. You will need it for the show times and your FASTPASS return times. Like most places it is cheaper to eat a breakfast or lunch. If you are staying at a Disney resort and using all their transportation, Uncle Walt owns all the restaurants you will go to. Eat a later breakfast and lunch, then a light snack later in the day will save you a few dollars.

Another very nice and fun feature you can do for your kids is in the area of EPCOT. If you are not aware EPCOT is divided into two general sections, Future World and World Showcase. Future World is the area with Space Ship Earth, or as everybody else calls it, the big golf ball. The World Showcase is divided into eleven countries from around the world. You can purchase your children a World Showcase EPCOT Passport in one of the stores in the World showcase. As you go from country to country, your children apply the appropriate stickers and give it to a representative of that country. They will stamp it and sign it with a personalized message, in their native language, to your child.

Your child can also get a paper facemask from one of the countries you visit. Your child colors it anyway they please. Then as you go from country to country your child receives a mask to cover only the eye area of the original mask. The stamp used for stamping the passports is then stamped on the stick to which the facemask is attached.

Something else we didn't do this trip, but that doesn't mean you shouldn't, is take an autograph book. There will be many times that you are looking to kill a little time in between shows. For example the Hall of Presidents only lets you in on the hour and the half hour. You probably don't want to get in line for another ride, but you want to keep the kids busy. Plus walking away from a character before you get an autograph is a lot better than getting out of line for a ride or attraction to get an autograph.

CHAPTER EIGHT: HOLIDAYS

Even for a happily married couple the holiday season can be very stressful, even more so for the divorced family. No matter how the division of holidays is done, being away from one parent during them is even more stressful on the children than on the parent. If the divorced parents live close to one another, it is easier to share most holidays. One parent can have the children on Christmas eve, the other on Christmas day, or one gets the children for Thanksgiving day they other spouse later in the weekend. Even if you give up the children for the entire holiday you will see them sometime around the holiday. If however one spouse lives some distance away the division of holidays gets more problematic.

Travel at any holiday is hard, but for unaccompanied minors it is something that must be planned in advance. If your children have to fly to the other parent, you can request the airline treat them as an "unaccompanied minor." An unaccompanied minor is a child under the age of 12 years old. You tell the airline you will have unaccompanied minors when you make the reservations. Make sure you get to the airport even earlier than normal as there are additional forms that must be filled out prior to your children being allowed on the plane.

This information includes the name, address, and phone number of the person at the arriving airport. You will also be asked for an alternate contact at the arriving airport. The first time I did this I didn't know this and was scrambling to find my ex-wife's address. I had no other phone number for the arriving airport for an alternate contact. Luckily I had my ex-wife's home phone number in my cell phone and could list it as the second contact phone number. Save your self some time and when you drop your children off the first time and ask for extra forms and fill them out in advance. You will also want to tell the ticket agent that you are dropping off non-accompanied minors. Sometime they will want you to go into a specific line, as you cannot use the self-serve feature most airlines are now offering.

Because of the new airport security protocols you will need to get a boarding pass for a non-ticketed passenger so you can walk your children to the gate. You will be required to stay at the airport until your children board the plane and the plane takes off. You and your children will still have to go through security like everybody else. So far I have found it easier to pack only carry on luggage. This is mainly for the parent picking up the child. It is easier to just pick your children up at the gate and go, than getting them at the gate then going to baggage claim and waiting for their luggage.

With the recent arrests and reported terror plots in the United Kingdom and the further restrictions placed on carry on items, I have even looked into the possibility of streamlining this process even more. You know where your children are going. Consider sending clothing and other personal items for them ahead via some other carrier. UPS, Federal Express, the United States Postal System or other ground or air carrier would do the trick just fine. This would work good even at Christmas with getting gifts back home. Waiting at baggage claim with tired children is not the most pleasant of experiences.

When you go to the airport to pick up your children arrive early again, as you will also have to go to the ticket counter and get a pass for security. Just arrive a little early and tell the airline the arriving flight number and your children's names. They will issue you the appropriate pass to get through security. Don't forget to take your ID.

Most airlines also only allow one adult per unaccompanied minor. I was caught up on this one once. The ticket agent gave both of my parents the non-ticketed voucher, while I was filling out the forms for Seth and Spencer, then refused to give me one because she had already given one per child out. It took me so long to convince the supervisor to let me go through too that by the time I got to the gate, the boys were already on the plane. The gate agents were nice enough to let me go onto the plane to say goodbye to the boys.

Before any of this takes place you should contact different airlines in your area to see what their policy is concerning unaccompanied minors. When it comes to your children flying by themselves, saving a few dollars may not be worth the aggravation you will be putting your children through. This might even include trying to get direct flights if possible, even if it is a few dollars more. Also consider when your children are getting back home.

I can understand wanting to spend as much time with your children as possible. But is it really fair to get back home at 9:00 or 10:00 at night? How about when there are time zone changes. You get your child to the airport at least an hour early, and then put them on their flight. There are rarely meals served on flights any more. By the time they get home it is too late to have dinner or you are eating very late. Keep in mind not only when your children will be leaving you, but what time will they be getting home. A later flight might be what you want, spending more time with them, but what is better for them?

In my case it may get even more involved. Because Seth will be twelve soon, he will no longer be considered a minor. That means that Spencer is no longer an "unaccompanied minor." He is traveling with a twelve-year-old adult. A twelve-year-old adult, I wonder who decided that? I guess I'll be burning that bridge when it gets here.

Now that that is out of the way, I will try addressing some general topics of some specific holidays. New Years Eve is an interesting holiday. Most of us probably don't want to take a child to your typical New Years Eve party. If you look you can find other, family alternatives. In my area the city of Annapolis offers a program called First Night Annapolis. This involves a variety of events and attraction like street performers, and musical acts. Most churches now also offer some type of evening service, with activities for your children. Sometimes we just go outside with the neighbors and let all the kids bang on pots with wooden spoons. Of course if your kids are young enough you may not have to worry about it. Maryland now allows what are called ground-based fireworks. These are really nothing more than fancy sparklers. I buy a few packs after the forth of July and keep them till January, another budget tip. That way we can have our own little firework display anytime we want to.

If they are traveling away for these two holidays, Christmas and New Years, remember they will be getting back home in just about enough time to go back to school.

The next big holiday is Easter. I am mainly going to mention the holidays that the children will be off of school and will probably therefore be split with the other parent. In our society Easter isn't celebrated with big parties, short of the occasional Easter egg hunt. So there will not have to be much planning on your part for something for your children to do. Much will rely on how you celebrate Easter, as a religious or secular holiday. You will have to look into the logistics of your children either flying or driving over what is a very busy traveling weekend. A lot of how Easter is split will depend on your children's school system. If they only get off Good Friday and Easter Monday, it will drastically cut into your visitation, if travel time is a factor. If however it is built into a spring break, you will have more leeway.

Through the course of the school year there will be any number of long weekends. These will probably be split between both parents if they live with in a closer or reasonable distance of each other. A three-day weekend is always nice. The main problem with these types of school breaks is that just because the school is closed, that doesn't mean the parent is off. You may have to plan even further in advance for these days as they are typically not what you would call traditional holidays.

Another thing is that it looks like more school districts are going to what they call year round school schedules. Instead of getting off through the entire summer, they go to school through the summer, but have more two week or so, long breaks throughout the school year. If your children are in this type of school you will have different requirements for scheduling their vacation visits with the "not at home" spouse.

Halloween is another big holiday, at least at our house even though children are rarely off school for it. In our area elementary schools have a day they call Book Character day. On that day your child wears their costume to school, but must bring a book about the character they are dressed like. If you are like me and on a fairly tight budget, you have to find ways to economize. This year Seth wanted to be the monster hunter Van Helsing, and Spencer wanted to be a pirate. To get both boys the costumes they wanted I took them to the local Goodwill and the local Salvation Army. We went through the clothes and were able to piece together complete costumes for both of them for about twenty dollars.

You will also have to face the issue of someone being at your house handing out candy, while your children are out Trick or Treating at other houses. Ben, their friend that moved, usually comes back and Trick or Treats with Seth and Spencer. Ben's parents go with them and I stay at the house.

I will address Thanksgiving and Christmas as one holiday season. For the most part you will only get one of these holidays; the other will be with the other parent. This year for example I will have the boys for Thanksgiving and they will be with their mother for the entire Christmas holiday this includes New Year. Besides the long visitation during the summer months, this wraps up three major holidays in a little over thirty days. These two need special consideration.

Retailers and our society in general start the Christmas holidays earlier and earlier every year. When I was a kid I remember the stores starting to decorate for Christmas the day after Thanksgiving. Then they started in November, now we don't even make it to Halloween before we see Christmas products and decorations out in stores. It is getting harder to separate them into separate holidays.

My plan this year is to try to get an artificial tree. We will put our Christmas tree up and decorate it during the Thanksgiving holiday just like the retailers. I will celebrate Christmas with the boys and my family a week before they leave to go out with their mother. That way I can have a Christmas for them here too. On the year I have the boys for Christmas and not Thanksgiving I will take them out for a "Thanksgiving" dinner the weekend after they get back from their mother's. It will be a nice, not crowded Thanksgiving dinner for us. Something I did one year as something different was I had Thanksgiving around the world. Instead of the traditional turkey and fixens we had tacos for Mexico, spaghetti for Italy, sour beef from Germany and orange chicken for China. My parents weren't that thrilled, but the kids thought it was great. For my non-Thanksgiving years this may become the standard.

Another budget idea is in Christmas shopping. If your children are young like mine, they like opening presents as much as what they get. For stocking stuffers and small gifts I go to the Dollar Store. I wrap them all so they have more gifts to open. Lets be honest, most toys are played with and broken or discarded a few days after Christmas anyway. A friend of mine once just got big boxes and filled them with construction paper, coloring books, crayons, and markers, all of which are available at your local Dollar Store. Of course they liked the big boxes as much as the stuff inside. This might be a good time to try to remind your children what these two holidays are supposed to be about anyway, not just Turkey and presents.

If your children are young enough to be concerned about such things, make sure they know that you have already filed a change of address at the North Pole with Santa so he will know whose house to take their presents to. This too will need some cooperation between parents. Santa knows to only give one gift, so if your children send off a list to Santa, be sure you share it with the other parent. There will also be some gifts that will stay at one parent's house even after the children leave.

My ex-wife and I for example split the different types of gaming platforms. They have a Game cube at their mother's house and a Playstation at my house. That way you don't run into the problem of games that one parent buys getting left or lost at the other's house. A nice feature with the Game cube is the games you buy for a hand held Gameboy can be played on the Game Cube with the purchase of an adapter.

Easter is another holiday that is usually split. Some school systems tie the Easter holiday into what is called a spring break. This break can be anywhere from four days to a week. It is of course up to you how you celebrate Easter, as a religious holiday or just another break from school. This too is usually a fairly heavily traveled holiday and the coordination between parents will need to be done in the best interests of the children.

If you are a single parent because of divorce, have custody of your children and your ex-spouse lives far enough away so that your children have a long travel time or a flight there is another thing to consider. I think it is very important for your children to go to school. But think about your children in the light of your situation. If your children have to fly or even go on an extended drive, remember everyone else is traveling those days too. This may be the time to allow your children to get out of school early or even miss a day. The traveling will be much easier for them and for you, if they aren't fighting all the other travel traffic, even if that means letting your ex-spouse have the children a day or so early.

To the non-custodial parent, maybe you should think about the same thing. Letting your children go home a day or two early will give them an easier time traveling. This is especially if the distance between the two residences involves time zone changes. Give them a few days to re-adjust to their time zone before they have to go back to school.

While not officially a holiday, birthdays have to be addressed too. Each of these presents their own unique difficulties. Seth's birthday is in March, the only month the boys don't have any days off school. It is next to impossible for his mother to be here for his birthday, and there are no long weekends near his birthday. Spencer's birthday is in August shortly before they start back to school. It would be unfair for Spencer's mother to get Spencer every year as part of her summer visitation picks. Yet she should be able to have part in the boy's birthdays.

An issue I have noticed is that Seth's birthday is during the school year, so he has school friends to invite to his birthday party. Spencer's birthday is during the summer, so there are no school friends to invite. Spencer was with his mother this year for his birthday so I had his later, after school started. Birthdays will have to be factored into visitation, just like every other holiday.

Mother's Day and Father's Day seem to take care of themselves. Celebrations for the parents' birthdays, and family birthdays will also have to be arranged between both parents.

So far I have addressed persons in my position of being a single male parent through divorce. As I mentioned earlier my friend Donald is a single parent through the death of his wife. This too presents some interesting holiday problems. In my case, if my ex-wife's family wants to talk to the boys they have my phone number and are free to call or come over anytime they like. Anytime the boys ask about them I will never tell them they can't see them. But as for structured visits, I believe it is my ex-wife's responsibility to keep the boys involved with her family members if she wants.

Donald, and all those in his position, are fully responsible not only for raising his children, but maintaining a relationship with both sets of grandparents, aunts, uncles and any other family members. This means splitting vacations, holidays, amicably with all the relatives involved. Donald has to have a holiday at his house for his children. Then he has two sets of grandparents to coordinate with for holidays and birthdays. This too is further complicated if there is a long travel time between these various relatives and where you live.

CHAPTER NINE: SHOPPING ON A BUDGET

Again I am just a retired police officer. I am not and economist or a professional shopper. It seems like in any family one spouse does all the shopping. Unfortunately, for the most part, it is the wife that is saddled with that job. In today's economy shopping is a job into its self. I have touched on some shopping earlier; I will go into a little more depth in this chapter.

As I addressed earlier most men are not that familiar with the grocery store. Now that you are a single parent, and supporting you and your children on less income than you were used to, you have to become what I like to call an aggressive shopper. We will cover groceries first.

There are some rules that will save you money and headaches in the future. First, never shop for food while you are hungry. You would be amazed at the junk you will pick up if you're hungry. You'll find yourself buying snacks and quick fixes you would normally never buy. You will either do that, or try to be done as fast as you can so you can go eat, doing that will cost you money too. Impulse buying is the mortal enemy of the family budget.

The second is to prepare a shopping list. We use a white board on the refrigerator when we run out of something, it goes on the list. The boys are allowed to write on this list as it makes them feel they have a say in what food we buy. Again you will be amazed how much junk you'll buy if you go through the store without a list.

Even with one, try go shopping and get only what is on the list. Also you will only have to spend all day shopping and putting away your goods, only to realize you have forgotten to get what you really went to get in the first place once to help you realize the importance of a list. Many married men will tell you stories of being sent to the store by their wife with a list. They come home proud to have fulfilled their husbandly duties and gotten everything on the list. Then the questioning starts. "Where is the milk? What about a loaf of bread?"

"They weren't on the list."

"You know we always get (insert any number of products here) every time we go shopping."

Well obviously you didn't or you would have brought it home. My example again is milk. We go through anywhere between four to six gallons of milk a month. You can't buy milk in the beginning of the month and have it last through the month. It is pretty safe for me to say that if we go to the store, we are coming home with a gallon of milk. In your house it may be something different, but there will be some product you run out of every week.

I can remember more than once the boys and I went to the store for a gallon of milk. The gallon of milk wound up costing us fifty or sixty dollars as we picked up other items while walked through the store. Another quick tip is if you are going in for one thing, say a six-pack of sodas. By the way they all seem to be twelve packs now. Go in the store and walk directly to the soda aisle, get your six-pack and leave. Also don't take in a cart. If you take in a cart you will do your best to fill it. If you have to carry everything, your arms will fill up much faster than your cart will.

I do the majority of my grocery shopping at BJ's wholesale club. I'm sure there is something like it near you. This store is similar to Costco or Sam's Club. There are several benefits to shopping at a store like this, but also several drawbacks. I like that you can do all your shopping for the month in one day. Of course if you do this, remember that it will take you almost as long to put the groceries away after you get home than it took you to buy them.

Remember the aggressive shopper I mentioned? Let me give you some specifics in my life. The price of a gallon of skim milk at BJ's wholesale club at my last trip was $2.09 a gallon. I buy two gallons at a time. At my local grocery store a gallon of skim is $2.69. The 7-11 down the street from me charges $3.29 for the same gallon. As you can see there are huge swings in the price of products from store to store. That is anywhere between a $1.20 to a $2.40 for the two gallons of milk.

As a general statement most of your staples like loaves of bread, milk, and paper products like towels, napkins, and toilet paper are cheaper at the wholesale clubs. The major drawback to these types of clubs is that you have to buy in bulk. By way of example on my last trip I bought paper towels. The "bundle" of paper towels has twenty rolls of paper towels. I bought Pop Tarts on this trip too. The box was four boxes of twelve or forty-eight Pop Tarts. There is certainly a storage issue to be considered in shopping at these types of clubs.

It is almost always cheaper to buy products in bulk. Make sure you have the storage for your products. Paper products you can put just about anywhere. Canned goods can also be stored about, but fresh and frozen foods have to be dealt with right away. Sometimes you can get a five-pound bag of chicken breasts pre frozen and separated in a bag. But your ten-pound package of pork chops will have to be opened and divided into meal-sized portions, before being frozen.

Sugar is best bought at the local grocery store. If you are going through the twenty-five pound bags at the wholesale clubs, then you should reevaluate how much you are putting in your morning coffee. Also products like rice, flour and alike often come in larger than needed for personnel use size.

If you can find another family that wants to split shopping you may be able to get some fantastic deals by buying some of these truly bulk items. Just be sure to keep track of what you bought and divide them up as soon as you are done shopping

If you can afford a second freezer, I would recommend it. On the farm I was raised on we had two freezers in the basement. One was only for meats, and one for vegetables and fruits. I have even checked with my local power company. Even they say if you are buying in bulk at lower prices, the cost of extra electricity is more than offset by the savings in the cost of the food.

No matter how well I do at the wholesale club, I always wind up going to the local grocery store, again another draw back to the wholesale clubs. The boys and I like to make quesadillas for dinner every now and then. When we make them, we don't need a ten-pound bag of shredded cheese to make quesadillas for two boys and one adult. So I buy small re-sealable bags of shredded cheese at the grocery store. I used to buy breakfast cereal at BJ's. I could get a box with two bags of cereal for about $6.00. At my local grocery store I could get two bags of "Fruity Loops" for $5.00. Let me address "Fruity Loops" in just a minute.

There are also things you almost can't buy at the warehouse stores. Like fresh fruit. Many times the prices are better at the local stores. Plus apples, pears, and bananas only stay fresh for so long. By the time you get around to finishing off the five pounds of fruit you bought at the ware house store half will be rotten or at least very over ripe.

The grocery budget often has to absorb many things that are not groceries. The biggest of these categories is cleaning supplies in general. There are several areas of clean supplies within the overall category of cleaning supplies. All of them seem to be disproportionally expensive. There are house-cleaning supplies, clothes washing supplies and personal hygiene products. I think the easiest way to budget for these products is to try not to have to by them all at the same time.

For example, if this month you buy laundry detergent, fabric softener, bleach, bleach alternative , dryer sheets or anything else you use for clothes washing. Hold off on buying other products. The good thing with cleaning products, unlike food, is they last longer than a few weeks. Try to keep ahead of these products. Buy house cleaning products another month and personal care products the third. Or like food replace them as soon as you either run out or use one.

On products I use for clothes washing, I try to keep an extra of everything. When I run out of say fabric softener, I have another to open. Then on my next trip I replace that one product. So far I have been lucky enough not to run out of both at the same time.

I also put paper towels napkins and toilet paper in this category. Remember to check the bathrooms for toilet paper. You don't have another adult to yell to if you are unable to complete the paperwork in the bathroom. This is another area where you want to replace the item as soon as you use it. We keep extra toilet paper under the sink, when a roll comes out, another goes in, well most of the time. Keep up on the hand soap in the bathrooms too.

In the olden days way back before my first marriage I owned a 1970 Chevrolet Corvette, 1970 corvette red. There was a running joke among all Corvette owners that when you needed a part the store would get the part and then add $5.00 for every letter in the word Corvette. Once I went to a local auto parts store and told the clerk that I needed a fuel pump for a 1970 Chevrolet 350 high performance engine. He looked in his book and said hold on. Went into the back and came out with my fuel pump, $27.00. I took it home and climbed under the car and noticed he had sold me the wrong one. I took it back and told him it was the wrong one. He asked again what I needed it for, I told him, and he said this is the right one. Then he asked me exactly what kind of car is this for? A 1970 Corvette. Oh, wait a minute. He put that book away and got out another one. Yup, you're right, that's not the one you need. The one you need is $129.00 and I can have it in a week.

That little story was told as a segue for this story. During that same time I found out that there were only a few manufacturers of tires in the country. The tires you bought at K-Mart might have been made by Uniroyal, or Good Year. The same is still true.

I needed a battery for my Excursion. I asked around and was told that Interstate Batteries were about the best around. I went to the local battery warehouse and told the guy what I needed and wanted. The honest salesman told me that Interstate was probably the best car battery around. However he had their store brand for about $30.00

less. Guess who made their battery? That's right; it was made by Interstate, just branded for my battery warehouse instead of Interstate.

All that was said to get to this fact. When you are in the grocery store, don't be a brand name snob. The grocery store where I shop is privately owned by Mr. Lauer. He owns two grocery stores in my area. Now they sell all the brand names like all stores. They also carry their own store brand of just about everything. You don't really think this man that owns and operates two grocery stores has his own canning and packaging factories for his stores? No his store brand is someone else's just branded with labels for his store. If you look carefully at the brand named product you just bought you will sometimes see "This formula is not sold to any retailer as a store brand." Gee now if they weren't doing it with other products , why have a message like that. Does that mean with some minor changes to the "formula" you can sell it as a store brand?

I'm sure this holds true for most stores. Remember earlier I mentioned the candle melters? Well a 22-ounce Yankee candle at your local craft or Yankee Candle store will run you about $22.00. At BJ's wholesale club I bought a 21-ounce candle for $8.99. I took it home and turned it over and guess what it said? The Yankee Candle Company Inc. In other words I can buy two for less than one of the brand name. In the grocery store I have no problem buying bags of "Fruity loops or Frosty Flakes" rather than something sold by the Toucan or the Tiger. They are at least $1.00 cheaper.

This even holds true for clothes. Target carried a brand of men's casual pants called Timberline. If you check the tag carefully, you'll see it reads Timberline by Wrangler. London Fog has an off name brand too, I'm sure most manufactures do.

Think of it this way. Most of us go to the pharmacy and order medicine for ourselves or our children. And we almost always say that generic will be fine. If generic is fine for the pills you take to keep your heart beating, then why pay extra for your breakfast cereal?

Another thing people talk about is coupons. I know that every now and then you see on the news about some one getting two grocery carts full of food and after coupons they pay $3.72. So it must therefore be possible. However I'm talking to a group of people that may have never shopped. Let's say you have a .50 coupon for brand X paper towels and with the coupon they now cost $4.50, but the everyday price for brand Y is $4.00. Which do you get? I say brand Y and save an additional .50 over brand X.

Some coupons are worth it though. I get Uncrustables by Smuckers for the boys for lunch. Now if I get a coupon for Uncrustables I use it, no one else makes them so I can't very well buy another, cheaper brand.

Watch out for buy one get one free deals. Often my grocery store offers buy one get one free deals on ice cream. If you buy ice cream at $5.25 for a half a gallon and get one free, that means they are about $2.62 ½ per half gallon. But another brand might only be $2.30 per gallon. Two of them would only be $4.60, which is the better deal?

Rebates are another ploy manufactures use to get you to buy their products. They say their product is only $15.00. That is of course after the $35.00 mail in rebate. This means you pay $50.00 for the product at the register. You then get to go home and fill out a form, copy your receipt, and find something on the box and send it in. Six to eight weeks later the manufacturer sends you a letter telling you that you sent the wrong part from the box, sorry no rebate. Of course by then you have thrown out all the original receipts and packing, so you can re-file it.

I have gotten some rebates back but for the most part I'm not a big fan of them. There are some rebates that are easier to use, and even some that are taken off right at the register. Overall though, I still think your best bet is to shop aggressively and look for the best value price before any coupon or rebate.

If you are trying to stretch your budget dollars buy getting those coupon books, look them over carefully before you buy them. Most of them offer a buy one-get one half-price deal. However it normally means two adult entries. As one of your kids get too old for the child's menu, they become a better deal. You will want to know your restaurant's children's policy. The ages can vary from ten and under to twelve and under. Most restaurants also offer some type of kids eat free night. Again remember most of the time that means per paying adult. Keep an eye of the clock, you don't want to miss the deal by being ten minutes early.

I mentioned earlier Dollar stores. Even there you have to be careful. Just because you are shopping at what is listed as a discount store doesn't mean everything there is the lowest price you can find. One hundred 4X6 index cards will cost you $1.00. Good price right? Well the same pack of 4X6 index cards at Wal-Mart was .49.

Various discount stores are in everyone's area. Stores like Marshall's, Ollie's, Value City or Big Lots buy surplus items. Many of their products are indeed still brand names. They might to be last year's model or discontinued products. Sometimes they are buyouts of excess orders or stores that have closed. Many stores sell discounted products because they sell seconds, or factory rejects. This could be something as small as a crooked seam on your pillowcase. It could also be something major, so make sure you look over what you buy to make sure the defect is something you can live with.

Another thing men, including myself, have to learn is when you should shop. Winter clothes seem to go on sale earlier and earlier. And summer clothes start earlier. If your kids need a winter coat, get it for them early, or wait till January or so and get a larger size for about half price.

If you are brave enough to try ordering things off the internet or from a catalog you can get some good deals there too. However if the size is wrong it is more complicated returning things by mail than returning them to the store. You will also need to learn that almost every store has a different return policy. Keep the receipt for everything you buy until at least your kids try on everything.

In the area of trying on things, if you can take your kids to the store do so. Everything appears to be cut differently, even within the same brand name. My boys and I wear for the most part, Wrangler jeans. They need one size in the cargo pants, but another size if they want the carpenter pants, unbelievable. The try on method, is much better than the, what size do you wear, method.

When you are in a store look around for unadvertised deals. Many stores will offer something free or greatly discounted with the purchase of a certain dollar amount. If you had planned to purchase that amount anyway, pick up a "gift" for little to no money. I pick up these items all year long, then at Christmas or birthdays I go into the basement and sort out what to give to whom. Many stores offer small free sample size products. One of these is a simply a sample product, but ten or fifteen of them becomes nice stocking stuffers if not an out right gift.

Something that may help you with this is to wait until January. Most stores will have storage containers with lids and all. Buy one for everyone you have to buy Christmas presents for. Put their name on the lid. Then throughout the year when you see something you think they would like get it and put it in their container. This will not only help with your budget, but you will know how much you have bought for each person. This is especially important if you have more than one child to buy gifts for.

I have found there is no one store that has the lowest price on everything. The best thing you can do is shop around and do your best. Remember if you pay less for everyday items you will have more to spend on your children. Kids of divorce want their parents. Don't worry so much about what you think brand names mean. Clean clothes, good food, and a safe environment with you will mean a lot more to them than designer names and less time with you.

CHAPTER TEN: THE GOOD TIMES

Ok we have been way too serious for way to long. I have mentioned several times already about the differences between men and women as single parents. There are other differences that I'll bring up now. Men, unlike women are used to and expect instant gratification. Women on the other hand have had to learn to wait for it. This is true in many areas. Now get your minds out of the gutters and take a walk with me.

Men only see the successes of parenting when the child grows up. What did they become? Did they finish college, did they go at all? Women see the everyday things that give them their parenting reward now. They don't have to wait for the child to grow up to see it. So men here is where you can find the instant gratification you seek.

Many men will never know the joys of the things your children do or say. This is unfortunately the cost of our dual income families. Men, it is also our fault. It is only when we are forced into single parenthood that we start to pay attention to our children. Sometimes after an especially hard day I start to think of some of the things they have done or said. You have to smile at the innocence that we all once had, but have given up in the name of becoming an adult. Remember you can't stop growing older, but no one said you had to grow up. I wanted to share some of the things I have gotten the pleasure of seeing and hearing my boys do.

One day while we were camping Seth, Spencer and their friend Ben were sitting on the couch in the trailer. Seth was karate chopping Ben and Spencer in the back. I asked him what he was doing. He said he was giving them a mirage. A what, I asked? You know daddy, a mirage. Now for those of you that don't speak little boy what he meant to say was that he was giving them a massage.

In our house snacks play an important part in our daily activities. I have the boys pick out their own snacks. If they pick out an inappropriate snack I say no and have them pick out another one.

At night once we were talking about what we wanted as a nighttime snack. Spencer told me he wanted ravens. Ravens what do you mean, ravens? You know daddy, ravens. Now keep in mind we live in Maryland just south of Baltimore. Our professional football team is the Baltimore Ravens. So again I'm trying to use my superior adult intelligence to figure out what type of football food he was talking about. Finally I gave up, no Spencer I have no idea what you're talking about, what is a raven. You know daddy those little black chewy things. They kind of look like a grape. Oh a raisin, OK that's fine.

On the weekends we have a little special breakfast. One day I asked Spencer what he wanted to have for breakfast. He told me he wanted a greasy egg. My mind started spinning. OK I have the egg part, but I was lost on the greasy part. What do you mean? You know a greasy egg. Well I'm thinking, an egg cooked in bacon grease? No we have never done that. We use turkey bacon and then still cook the eggs in a second pan. Spencer, I still don't know what you mean, I don't know what a greasy egg is. You know the kind of egg that you stick your toast into the greasy part. He was talking about what we call a dippy egg, this would be either a sunny side up or an over easy.

Once my daughter came over and like all college kids her age she promptly fell asleep on the couch. Spencer was getting hungry as it was close to time for supper. Now if Spencer is hungry it is time to eat right now. Spencer was having trouble waking her up, so he did like all of us would do, he picked up her shoe and threw it at her. "Well I just wanted to wake her up to ask her if she wanted anything to eat for supper." What a thoughtful, caring brother.

One day Spencer came home from school and he was upset. He told me a boy on the bus had hit him on his hand. I asked Seth what had happened. He told me Spencer and the other boy had both reached for the seat back at the same time as they got up to get off of the bus. The other boy's hand hit Spencer's hand. Clearly this was just an accident, but that didn't make Spencer any less upset. So Spencer and I went into his room to talk. It ended with him saying he wanted a hug. He said that's what daddies are for. I said ok and gave him a hug. Then I asked him for one and asked him if daddies are for giving hugs, what are little boys for. He thought about it and said, "To aggravate their daddies." I didn't even know he knew that word, much less what it meant. Of course I thought if that is what little boys are for, you're doing a bang up job of it alright.

Another thing that I have come to like is nighttime. Spencer plays hard all day long, and when it is time to go to sleep he just crashes. I have some great pictures of him asleep. Again I will welcome all to have a laugh at my expense. My mother tells me I was the same way. She says I would play hard for days, then quit. She had a picture of me where I walked up to the couch, laid my head across the cushions and fell asleep there, standing up.

I have pictures of Spencer sleeping on the floor, at the bottom of the steps, sitting up at the kitchen table and sitting in a chair watching TV. As a side note I would recommend any parent to take as many embarrassing pictures as possible of your children. That way when they get rich or become the President of the United States, they will be more than happy to take care of their old dad.

Once, Spencer's fingernail got infected. After soaking it in Epson salts, clipping it short so it wouldn't catch on anything, it was still obvious that the nail would come off. Spencer was upset and started crying, so I tried to console him. I told him that it wasn't a big deal, that is was just like when he lost a baby tooth. I told him another one would grow in to take its place. He thought about what I had said for a while and then asked, "Well if I put it under my pillow will I get money?" I knew I couldn't laugh at him but I had to say something. So I just told him no, that the tooth fairy doesn't do that, and that there wasn't a fingernail fairy.

Now speaking of the tooth fairy I had an episode with Seth. In our family we try not to spend our change. I get the quarters and the boys split the other coins. Well as you might imagine, that gives the tooth fairy lots of quarters, but makes the tooth fairy a little reticent to part with his quarters, back to the story. Seth lost a tooth and the tooth fairy was real busy and tired and didn't make it to his pillow. I told Seth sometimes the tooth fairy is very busy and to put it back under his pillow again.

The tooth fairy felt bad about it the next night and when he paid a visit he left a dollar for the tooth, and left feeling pretty good about himself. The next day Seth got up and I asked him if the tooth fairy had made it to his bedroom last night. He looked a little sad so I thought maybe he didn't find the dollar. He looked at me and told me that the tooth fairy came but left a dollar. He said he wanted a quarter not a dollar. Sometimes the tooth fairy can't win for losing.

Now I have to admit that the tooth fairy could use a refresher course because that wasn't the last time he forgot a tooth. Once Spencer lost one and put it under his pillow. The next morning he came into my room early and seemed upset. I asked him what was wrong. He told me that the tooth fairy didn't give him any money last night. I said that he must be mistaken and I would help him look. We went into his room and started looking. Instead of putting it under one of his big pillows, he put it under a small pillow at the foot of the bed, that tooth fairy he's such a kidder.

Now in case you haven't noticed yet I try to keep the little bit of sanity I have by interjecting humor into things. As I said earlier I try to keep the boys involved with activities and invite their friends to go with them. I have already mentioned their friend Ben. They are friends with the next-door neighbor, Nick. Now Nick is the same age as Seth, a little olive tone to his skin, like Seth, but has jet-black hair. I have been out with the four of them and hear people say something like this. Oh you could never deny those two, they look exactly like you. They are of course talking about Seth and Nick. Your other two must look like their mother, being Spencer and Ben.

Now Ben looks as much like his father as Seth looks like me. I have been out with the three of them, Seth, Spencer and Ben and people will say, you can't deny those two, Seth and Spencer, but your other one must look like his mother. You want to see a strange look on someone's face? That is when you look kind of sad, and hurt and say, no he looks like his father, come on boys lets go. I know it's bad, but you do get some good looks.

In every family where there is more than one child, you will see how different they are. They pick different friends and do different things. One day I was picking up some clothes in Spencer's room when I saw his friend Ryan's clothes laying on the floor, they were soaked. Spencer, what happened to Ryan's clothes? Oh he fell into a puddle so I gave him some of mine to wear. I didn't think much of it, and threw Ryan's clothes into the washer.

Things were fine until my neighbor came home. I guess I should have asked where a puddle was that was so deep that Ryan could fall into it, and soak all his clothes. Did I mention that my neighbors have a nice little fishpond in their back yard? Well guess whose boys had gone fishing in the fishing pond. Let us be nice and say that my neighbor was not amused to find that fishing season was in on his coy fish. Better yet that the little statues he had surrounding the pond must have tried to catch them too. However the fish were so much bigger than the statues, that their fishing rods were pulled right out of their little hands, we never did find them.

As I mentioned earlier I feel going to church is an important part of every family. I also mentioned that we try to go out to dinner after church. One day after church we stopped a Sunny's Surplus. That is a store that sells camping supplies. As we were leaving a large SUV pulled into the parking place next to us. Out of the SUV got a huge man with long hair and a long beard. Seth looked up at him and said "Look, Daddy, it's Jesus!"

Now it isn't just the boys that provide you with unexpected

moments. I try to expose my boys to as many different things and experiences as possible. My family has a strong German heritage. My father was born in Germany. There is a small German restaurant near Annapolis. It is called The Old Stein Inn, and bills its self as a beer garden in true German tradition. One day I took the boys there for dinner. I explained to out waiter I was there so the boys could try some different foods. I ordered the meal by pointing to items on the menu so the boys would have no idea what I was ordering them.

I ordered potato pancakes as an appetizer. It was served in traditional German fashion. You eat your potato pancakes with a dish of applesauce. In the dish of applesauce there is a cinnamon stick that you use to spread the applesauce over your pancakes. For our main meal I ordered two different types of German sausages. They cut them in half so each boy could try some of each. I told them they were just German hotdogs.

Not being one to let a sleeping hotdog lie, I decided to try something else. One afternoon I took the boys to a local Bennigan's. When we got inside there was a chalkboard listing the day's specials. Included on the list was an appetizer I knew we had to try. Again I explained to our server what I was trying to do and ordered by pointing at items on the menu. Our appetizer was delivered with a few different dipping sauces and we all dug in. I asked the boys if they liked it. They said yes they liked the onion rings I had ordered and told me which dipping sauce they preferred. I waited till we were done and they had eaten their meals before I told them they had not devoured onion rings. Our appetizer was calamari. At first they acted like kids, yuck! After I reminded them how much they liked it even they had to admit they liked it. They couldn't wait to tell their friends and my parents they had eaten squid.

As I have said I try to keep the boys involved in activities and with other kids, mostly their friends Ben and Nick. The school they go to and the area we live in is fairly diversified. My boys and hopefully their generation see only a friend to play with. Race seems to have no bearing on them at all. Once I was taking the four musketeers to the Washington Zoo. As we entered Washington I could hear them talking from the back of the car. They were discussing the people they saw. This was probably the first time any of them had been in Washington DC. The topic was do you have to be black to live in Washington DC. Why don't they let white people live there? As we continued into the city, one would say look there is a white person, yea there is another. I guess they will let anyone live in Washington. About that time the conversation changed slightly. This is the conversation I hear coming from the back. Seth, what color is your dad? Yea he isn't really white, but he isn't black either. Seth said I know, he's kind of tan colored. Again I couldn't laugh, but it was nice to hear all four of these boys apparently see skin color as nothing more than a descriptor, like hair or eye color.

In our school district every year in January the High school students are given standardized tests. During this week the boys' Elementary school closes two hours early Monday through Thursday and is closed on Fridays. The school the boys go to plans little special events every day during this shortened week. Monday was matching day. One of Seth's friends called him Sunday evening to plan what they would wear to match each other. Tuesday was crazy sock day. Spencer has a few pair of very brightly colored and loudly designed socks. He chose one of each so they would be mismatched. Now the school sent home a letter explaining dos and don'ts of this spirit week. They mentioned that on crazy sock day you had to wear shoes.

Well Spencer got dressed and started to roll up the cuffs of his pants. I asked him what he was doing. He said, I'm rolling up my pants so you can see the craziness. All I could think was, son you don't have to roll up your pants for anyone to see the craziness in you.

Maryland has quite a few nice State parks, one of which in Western Maryland is Cunningham Falls. We went there for a day trip over their Easter vacation. We went to one of the sections and there is a small aviary. It had about eight different types of birds that are native to Maryland. There were several types of owls, a few falcons, and buzzards. The star attraction was an American Bald Eagle. It was a six-year-old female, and we were standing only about four feet from her.

We then met up with my cousin and started to drive to the other side of the park, the side with the waterfall. Several years earlier a tornado had gone through the park and downed many trees. My cousin and I were mentioning about all the downed trees and remarking about all the huge exposed boulders. Spencer heard us talking and gave us his view on what must have happened.

He told us that maybe they knocked down the trees when they brought in all the rocks.

"Who knocked them down, Spencer?" I asked.

"The men that brought in all those rocks. I bet it was hard getting them on top of the mountain so they could roll them down," he replied.

For the rest of the trip we would mention the bigger rocks and he would tell us they must have used a tractor-trailer to bring them in.

The area we live in is northern Anne Arundel County, just south of Baltimore City. Most of the residents of the northern part of the county get our water from the Baltimore city water department. The 64-inch water main that comes from Baltimore city into Anne Arundel County broke one summer. The County Executive put a ban on all outdoor water usage. I was explaining to Spencer there was a water ban and that we couldn't wash the truck or water the yard or the flowers. As we were talking about this Seth was drawing bath water. Spencer said that Seth couldn't do that. I tried again to explain that it was outdoor uses that were banned. So he asked if we could use water guns outside. I said no Spencer where would you get the water. Stupid me I'm assuming the hose, right? Spencer said we could get the water from inside and then take it outside, that way we aren't using the outside water.

Seth and Spencer are very different in the morning too. Seth gets up before his alarm goes off. Makes his bed, gets dressed, and goes down stairs. I need a crow bar and three horses to get Spencer up in the morning. One day Seth got up and was already downstairs. I went into wake up Spencer. He stayed covered up with the sheets and blankets. I played the old "oh no, I don't see Spencer, where is he?" game. He kept quiet and kept the covers pulled tight over his head. I finally said, "Spencer, if you don't get up, you can't go to school. If you don't go to school everyone will miss you." Then, like a true child of the twenty-first century, he uncovered his head and said, "I'll just send a hologram." He then rolled over and covered back up.

Now clearly parenting isn't all about telling funny stories. Sometimes things get a little hectic. I was telling a friend one day that from about 6:00 PM till they go to sleep, it is almost nonstop, daddy, daddy, daddy, daddy. I told him I was going to change my name and not tell them what it was. He then told me this little parenting story.

Jim played in a little garage band. He told me they had a blind drummer and that from time to time as the venue permitted, the drummer's wife would bring their children to hear their father play. He said the first time they did, he thought he heard the children call their mother Debbie. He thought he must have heard them wrong and went on. The next time she brought them they again seemed to be calling her Debbie. This time he thought maybe it was a mispronunciation of some sort. Like if father was "daddy" maybe mommy was "Debbie." Finally it was too much for him and he worked up enough nerve to ask his drummer.

He said the drummer started laughing and told him this story. He said that his kids would "mommy" his wife half to death every night. One night in frustration she yelled, "Stop that, my name is Debbie!" Well like I said earlier, be careful what you tell your children.

One day Spencer and I were watching a music channel. As they played songs they would show little facts about the song, the band, and the year the song was released. Spencer would look at the year the song came out and ask me if I was alive then. I would answer if I was alive or I his uncle or mother had been born by then. The he asked me how old I was. I told him how old I was and he asked, "Daddy, have you had a heart attack yet?" I wanted to say something like, "Yes, and he is sitting on the couch." I said no, why? He told me that they told him in school if you don't have a heart attack before you're fifty years old you should live to be one hundred years old.

I had put the boys to bed one night and then went to bed myself. Around 1:30 something woke me up. I looked down the hall and the TV in Spencer's bedroom was on. Now I have woken up late at night and turned on the TV if I couldn't sleep, but I couldn't believe Spencer would. Every other time he has woken up at night he comes in my room with me. So I went down the hall to check on him. There was Spencer sound asleep with his TV on. He had gone to bed with the remote to his TV somewhere in his bed. He rolled over on it and turned on the TV. I looked for the remote but it was lost in the recesses of his bed sheets. I turned his set off the old fashion, you know by pushing the button. Spencer never even rolled over.

I was working one night with Seth on some extra hard spelling words, when I noticed it was too quiet again. Where was Spencer? I started looking around the house. Start in the kitchen, nope. Go through the family room, well it was a mess, but still no Spencer. I kept looking through the house. Where could he be? Well I finally found my little angel sound asleep, on the toilet.

Now in Spencer's defense he may not be able to help himself. There may be some genetic code predisposing him to this type of behavior. Remember the plastic saw story? Well as a little boy I refused to take naps. I had to play and play and play. My mother tells me that every three days or so, things would get quiet, too quiet and she would go looking. She still has pictures of me about Spencer's age. I am standing up with only my head on the living room couch, sound asleep.

I remember there was an add for a popular camera and film manufacturer. The picture used was that of a very large burly looking man with a little baby asleep on his hair-covered chest. There have been nights where either Seth or Spencer asks me to hold them. Seth sometimes asks me to stay with him for a while. Now I don't mean sleeping with them all night long. There have been nights when Seth was having a hard time falling asleep. I would lie in his bed, but set a time limit on it. He knew I would stay with him until a preset time. If the time comes and he is still awake, he has never complained when I get out of bed, but he does always check the clock to make sure I stayed as long as I said I would. It was OK with him that I got up, just as long as I stayed as long as I said I would.

Any father out there, single parent or not, that has not had one of their children fall asleep on their chest, or had one ask you to stay with them "just till I get sleepy," has missed out on one of the greatest parenting experiences there is.

Seth frequently does this. We will be watching TV, telling stories, or just talking and I can tell he is getting tired. He will say, "Daddy, can I just rest my eyes?" Sometimes as we lay there he will ask me if I still have my eyes closed. When your child has a bad dream and screams "Daddy" in the middle of the night, these are some of the instant gratification rewards you get when you work at being a father. No one will ever see or know about them, no one but you.

It was about 1:00 in the morning and I heard one of the boys get up and go to the bathroom. I thought if it is Seth he'll go back to bed, if it is Spencer, he'd be getting in bed with me soon. The light went off in the bathroom and I heard footsteps go down the hall. Well that means it was Seth and I rolled over. Then I heard the back door open. Oh no! Did someone break into the house and now I'm hearing them leave? I went downstairs to check the house. As I got downstairs I heard the TV. Maybe it was Seth having trouble sleeping. As I got to the family room, I saw Seth sitting on the couch dressed for school. He had let the dog out and opened the blinds on the slider.

"Seth, what are you doing?"

"Trying to find something to watch on TV."

"Why did you get up so early?"

"It was 6:00 so I got up and got dressed."

After I explained to him it was only 1:15, five hours till 6:00, he just looked up and said, "Well I'll just go back to bed." He got up, went upstairs, put on his pajamas and went back to sleep. Oh, to be able to go to sleep as fast as my kids.

One day, I was cleaning the family room. I was dusting behind the TV, stood up too fast, and hit my head on the corner of the fireplace mantle. I could feel I had broken the skin, and of course my pride. Later that day I asked Spencer to look to see if my head had stopped bleeding. He said that it had and that he could see where I had hit my head. "There's no blood, but you have a bald spot right back here." Thanks, Spencer, just what I needed to know.

One day, we were in BJ's, I had both boys with me, and we were heading to the check out line. We noticed a lady with a very full cart, you know the one just kind of standing there eyeing up the lines to see which one to get into. Well I looked at her and got her attention and asked if she was in line and was she going to the specific line I was headed for. She said she wasn't in line, that she was waiting for a friend to finish shopping, that they were going to check out together. I said thank you and got into line.

Spencer asked me why I asked the lady before we got in line. I tried to explain to him it was like when he was in line at the bus stop. If he was first in line, he wouldn't want someone coming up behind him and just getting in line in front of him would he? I told him I was just trying to be nice and polite and to think about other people, not just ourselves. I didn't really give it any more thought and finished our check out. We stopped at the food court and got a big soft pretzel and a soda.

From behind me I heard someone say excuse me. I thought maybe we were in someone's way so I moved the cart closer to our table. Again "excuse me." This time I turned around to see two women standing there. I recognized one of them as the woman I had asked about being in line or not. She stepped forward and began telling me how impressed she was that I would take the time to tell my boys the importance of polite conduct.

I am not trying to make myself out to sound like father of the year here. I know I am far from it. But if you want and still need some instant male gratification, you can still get it. I felt so good that someone actually noticed the time I was taking with the boys; what a feeling of accomplishment.

Earlier I mentioned how people would say what a good job I was doing and questioned if it was meant as "what a good job for a man." When you see a single parent out with their children and they are well behaved, tell the parent so. If you are in church or a movie and when you get up to leave and it is only then you realize you have been sitting in front of two children, tell the parents how good their children were. This is nothing more than something that if it isn't dead it is on life support; it is called polite society.

114

There is no need to wait till your children reach college or get their first job to see how they turn out. You will receive little reminders every day. The little things you do and say shape your children without you even knowing it. When you hear your child saying "excuse me" to a total stranger. When at the parent/teacher conference at school your child's teacher goes out of their way to tell you over and over again how polite you child is. There can be no greater reward to the trials of parenthood than these little comments made about you and your children.